The Compassionate Temperament

Postmodern Social Futures
Stjepan Mestrovic, Series Editor

Ways of Escape (1994), by Chris Rojek
Reluctant Modernity (1998), by Aleš Debeljak
Feeling and Form in Social Life (1998), by Lloyd E. Sandelands
Provocateur (1999), by Anthony J. Cortese
Civilization and the Human Subject (1999), by John Mandalios
Sociology after Bosnia and Kosovo (2000), by Keith Doubt
The Compassionate Temperament (2000), by Natan Sznaider

Forthcoming:

Agency and Power, by Blasco José Sobrinho
Science as Metaphor, Knowledge as Democracy, by Donald R. LaMagdeleine

The Compassionate Temperament

Care and Cruelty in Modern Society

Natan Sznaider

ROWMAN & LITTLEFIELD PUBLISHERS, INC.
Lanham • Boulder • New York • Oxford

ROWMAN & LITTLEFIELD PUBLISHERS, INC.

Published in the United States of America
by Rowman & Littlefield Publishers, Inc.
4720 Boston Way, Lanham, Maryland 20706
http://www.rowmanlittlefield.com

12 Hid's Copse Road
Cumnor Hill, Oxford OX2 9JJ, England

British Library Cataloguing in Publication Information Available

Library of Congress Cataloging-in-Publication Data

Sznaider, Natan, 1954–
   The compassionate temperament : care and cruelty in modern society / Natan
Sznaider.
      p.   cm. — (Postmodern social futures)
   Includes bibliographical references and index.
   ISBN 0-8476-9555-7 (cloth : alk. paper) — ISBN 0-8476-9556-5 (pbk. : alk. paper)
   1. Altruism.   2. Caring.   3. Helping behavior.   4. Civilization, Modern.
I. Title.   II. Series
HM1146 .S95   2000
303.4—dc21   00-055256

Printed in the United States of America

∞™ The paper used in this publication meets the minimum requirements of American
National Standard for Information Sciences—Permanence of
Paper for Printed Library Materials, ANSI/NISO Z39.48-1992.

For Yfaat and Shira

Contents

Acknowledgments

To be an intellectual is of course to be vastly indebted, both to one's friends and to innumerable authors. But to pay the intellectual debts incurred by this particular book I think a shorter list will suffice.

First and foremost comes Allan Silver. This book started as a dissertation under his guidance, based on his insights and fostered by his vast erudition. Had I not met him, I would not have written it. Second is my friend Michael Pollak, who listened to me expound these ideas in the intervening years when no one else would. My school, the Academic College of Tel Aviv–Yaffo in Israel, has been a wonderful place to work, and I am grateful that it allowed me the freedom to develop courses built around these ideas. My students there have consistently goaded me to clearer formulations. Special thanks go to its former president, Professor Elazar Kochba.

And last but not least, I would like to thank the editor of this series, Stjepan Mestrovic, a prolific author in his own right, for discovering me.

Portions of some of these chapters have appeared in different form in the following: "The Sociology of Compassion: A Study in the Sociology of Morals," *Cultural Values*, vol. 2 (1998), 117–39; "Pain and Cruelty in Socio-Historical Perspective," *International Journal of Politics, Culture and Society*, vol. 10 (1996), 331–54; "Compassion and Control: Children in Civil Society," *Childhood*, vol. 4 (1997), 223–40; "Democracy and Child Welfare," *International Journal of Politics, Culture and Society*, vol. 11 (1997), 325–50; "Compassion or Rights: The Case of Child Abuse," *New Political Science*, vol. 36/37 (1996), 69–87.

Introduction

Compassion—the organized campaign to lessen the suffering of strangers—is a distinctly modern form of morality. It played a historically important role in the rise of modern society, and it continues to play an important role today. And if we understand the nature of compassion and its connection to social structure, we can explain many social movements today that otherwise seem accidental, unprecedented, and postmodern.

The idea that the sight of suffering imposes a duty to ameliorate it seems like it should be a very old notion but is in fact a very recent one. There is a big distance between a duty that once bound saints and one that is now considered incumbent on all reasonable people. So little was suffering considered an evil before the nineteenth century that the guardians of morality paraded the spectacular suffering of evildoers before the public as a means of improvement. Public hangings continued until the end of the eighteenth century. And during the Reformation, often thought of as the first turning on the road toward modernity, people whose only crimes were doctrinal were routinely burned in the city squares of Europe's capitals.

The movement to reform such cruelties reflected a change in the conception of human nature. No longer were public displays of cruelty thought to be salutary. They were thought rather to be brutalizing—to the people who watched them. The idea that we must remove "brutalizing" conditions in order to "civilize" people developed in tandem with the development of capitalism. Coeval with the rise of capitalism and its "dark satanic mills," as William Blake described it, was a qualitatively new outpouring of compassion.

Compassion is the moral self-organization of society. It is the first moral campaign not organized by the church or the state. The structures of modernity are what make this self-organization of society possible. And the moral sentiments that result from this process constitute qualitatively new social bonds.

My argument in a nutshell is that it is in the nature of modernity to foster compassion. Despite the historical record, this is a minority view among today's

1

intellectuals. Most tend to think of modernity as corrosive of moral sentiments. They see clearly the way in which modernity breaks down older social bonds, but they are much less attentive to the way in which it builds new ones. And when waves of compassion break out into demands for political action, they are forced to consider it an atavism, an excuse, a subterfuge, or an irrelevancy.

There are many ways to make the argument that modernization corrodes compassion rather than increasing it and making it normal. Although I will deal with many authors (and especially with historians, since much of the work is empirically based), my main theoretical foils in this book will be Hannah Arendt and Michel Foucault. In the first place, their indictments of modernity are the most original. They are not mere recyclings of the *Gemeinschaft/Gesellschaft* distinction that is to be found at the base of so much other antimodernism. But more important, their arguments are the best of their kind. They fasten on the most difficult empirical issues and carry out their premises to their logical conclusions. In so doing, they raise the most crucial objections to my own argument. And lastly, they have been the most influential. It will take only a small amount of intellectual history to show that Arendt was as influential for the postwar generation as Foucault was for the generation that rebelled against it.

In the large outlines, I agree with the Foucauldians in characterizing the premodern era as one of "punishment," of exemplary cruelty. I also follow them in seeing an intellectual and experiential break between that era and our own (although I differ from them on almost every detail of how that break came about). And I applaud them for putting the institutions of social control at the center of the analysis of society. But where we part company is on our characterization of the present. What they see as discipline, I see as compassion. Where they see power, I see moral sentiments. And where they see social control as the state's control over society, I see social control as society's control over itself—a kind of control explicitly different from state control or religious control.

What the Foucauldians ignore, on principle, is the experience of people. Under the first regime, people are capable of taking their children to a public hanging as if it were family entertainment. Under the second, they feel queasy about violence on TV. The hypocrisy of the second case—the fact that, despite our queasiness, there is lots of violence on TV—should not obscure the sea change it represents: real physical violence—not the regulated violence of sports, nor the unreal violence of the cinema—makes modern people shiver with disgust. To simply hear the details of torture narrated produces in most moderns a physical revulsion. Sometimes it leads to outrage and clamoring that something must be done; sometimes it leads merely to the desire to switch the channel. But what it does not lead to is laughter and a feeling of satisfaction. And when it does—when we encounter people who enjoy killing, or people whom we feel have to be killed—it requires explaining. That is to say, we encounter it as an exception, as something that needs to be reconciled with our worldview.

This shift, from people—and societies—that reveled and prided themselves on killing and torture to societies that feel the pain of others so much that they have to hide it away or crusade against it is essential. The Foucauldians miss it, ironically, because they focus on continuities. It is true that there are still torturers in the world. But they are at the margins where they used to be in the center. They are hidden where they were once paraded. They are the exceptions where they used to rule. And this signifies a change both in how we experience the world and in how the world is.

The Foucauldians ignore this softening of manners as an epiphenomenon. I treat it as of central importance. In my view, it is not only the effect of structural changes, it contributed to the acceleration of those changes. And it is one of the keys to understanding the interaction between changing social structure and changing human nature. On my reading, Foucauldian theory has two main shortcomings: a concept of power that seems to have neither actors nor responsible parties; and a concept of state stretched so thin that it is in the end coextensive with the society that it pervades. I will argue that the concept of society as constituted by moral sentiments overcomes both these problems in the best possible way, preserving their insights while resolving their contradictions.

In the case of Hannah Arendt, the clear source of her idea that modernity is haunted by evil is the Holocaust. She is not alone in this; the attempt to explain how such a horror could possibly occur in a modern society defined social theory for thirty years afterwards, and its effects are still felt today. We could simply throw out this complex theory as misguided by saying that Arendt and others made the exception into the rule. But an exception that killed tens of millions of people, that forced Europe to give up its empire, and that divided a continent and history itself into two halves—this is not the kind of exception you can just ignore, especially if your theme is compassion. And especially when we consider that genocide is continually recurring, or threatening to recur, and that it bears the same relation to late twentieth-century movements of compassion as social questions bore to those of the early nineteenth century. So if we refute Arendt's theory, we are left with the problem she devised it to solve. A theory that maintains that normalized compassion is a logical outgrowth of modernity must explain why such massive exceptions do not in fact negate our interpretation. If we do not in the end make the Holocaust the model for modernity, we still have to take it seriously as the ultimate limit case. When the "Barbaric Temperament" is more than obvious, I think, a sociological and historical case can be made for the other side, namely the "Compassionate Temperament." Both are part of our world, but whereas it seems that modern intellectuals display more curiosity about barbarism, compassion is being forgotten or even ridiculed. This study seeks to set the record straight.

The first chapter will describe the historical and theoretical emergence of compassion in eighteenth-century Europe. I will examine the writings of some of the leading thinkers in this respect, believed to have laid the blueprints of the modern free market and modern democracy. Those thinkers, especially of the Scottish Enlightenment, thought that the necessary complement to these new social structures was a revolution in morals. This side of their argument was by far the most prominent at the time they wrote. Adam Smith, for instance, was considered chiefly a moral philosopher until seventy-five years after his death; it was only in the mid to late nineteenth century that he gained his reputation as a groundbreaking economist. Yet today, his *Theory of Moral Sentiments* has vanished from the consciousness of even well-read people. Another teacher of compassion, Rousseau, wrote novels that dealt almost exclusively with moral questions, were the greatest best-sellers of all time up to that point, and had vast popular influence during his lifetime and immediately afterwards. But *The Social Contract*, for which he is most remembered today, was largely a matter for specialists until much later.

In both cases, their moral arguments add a new dimension to their economic and political arguments. Neither author thought that a society of pure self-interest was possible. But neither did they think that self-interest, whether economic or political, was an acid that needed to be buffered by inherited norms. On the contrary, Smith and Rousseau welcomed the new systems of self-interest largely because they thought they would transform inherited norms into something better: away from the hierarchical ideals of honor, and toward the ideals of equality and moral universalism. Their arguments furnish the best starting point for understanding the relation between the two halves of modernization, the coevolution of interests and norms. Historically, the event usually considered the beginning of modernity was the French Revolution. It also plays a key role in the history of compassion. It produced the Declaration of the Rights of Man, perhaps the founding document in the history of human rights, and in its armies the ideal of equality literally conquered Europe. But the French Revolution was also the site of horrific cruelty. How can these two things be reconciled? Hannah Arendt gives a direct answer: compassion has no place in politics, and when it enters, it leads to cruelty. She believes that modernity begins with the mob of the French Revolution, and climaxes in the mobs of totalitarianism. I will dispute her interpretations of history, Rousseau, and the nature of compassion, and use that discussion to throw my historical argument into relief.

The next chapters will deal with the emergence of humanitarian consciousness during the eighteenth and nineteenth centuries. They will focus on the attempt to reform the lives of poor children (based on original research of mine) but will also discuss the campaigns to reform prisons and hospitals, the attempts to abolish slavery and torture, and other campaigns of compassion. These campaigns share so many essential similarities that in the end they can all be considered particular instances of the same broad social movement. Pain and the fight against its perceived evilness will organize my discussion. The pain of children is a good example of how compassion and innocence and purity are connected. Humanitarian movements delegitimized earlier values and practices and set up a new moral code in their place. Cruelty became understood as the infliction of suffering without the old justification for it, and compassion in organized form a public response to this evil. In the end, political action was not simply a reaction to social problems—it "created" the problems by changing the moral code. And the solution to these problems was undertaken just as much to affirm and solidify this new moral order as to solve the problems of social engineering. An important aspect of this study will deal with the relationship between humanitarianism and the emergence of liberal society, focusing on its distinctive features of capitalism (the market) and democracy (civic equality and citizenship). I will try to press beyond the purported inconsistency between the compassion of liberal sentiments and the individualism of liberal society to show their interdependence.

A book like this cannot ignore the breakdown of compassion. The Nazis' attempt to destroy European Jewry will serve as the limit case for the argument that modernity fosters the growth of compassion.

The relation between compassion and nationalism will also be explored in depth. Is nationalism the core reality of modernity—a moral universalism with boundaries? And is partial universalism worse than none? Is it simply tribal morality blown up to a horrific scale? Is there a reality to the "promise" of modernity in light of the heinous crimes of nations?

In the end I will try to draw the discussion together and analyze the tension between compassion and cruelty in modern society. I will try to understand the moral foundations of modern society as the interplay between compassion and barbarism that results from the world moving between a communal morality and a universal one.

This is also why I will try to reconstruct the voices of the "compassionate" reformers themselves. Their voices need to be heard in order not to sink into the cynicism of nihilistic rejection of compassion as moral sentiment.

Chapter 1

The Sociology of Public Compassion

What follows tries to provide a theoretical basis for a sociological study of compassion. Compassion involves an active moral demand to address others' suffering. Directed toward those outside the scope of personal knowledge, it becomes public compassion, shaping moral obligations to strangers in the arenas of civil society and liberal democracy. A sociological study of compassion clarifies the historical processes through which compassion for others' suffering shapes the definition of "social problems" and investigates the means by which specialists in organizing moral sentiments strive to alleviate the sufferings of others (Nisbet 1961). The sociological study of compassion requires exploration of the social and historical conditions that make this moral state possible. It investigates the manifestations of compassion in organized activity, expressing a moral state in action. In the case of compassion in liberal society, it involves not only action but a strong belief in universal benevolence, optimism, and the idea that happiness can be achieved in this life on earth, namely humanitarianism. A nineteenth-century humanitarian reformer concisely described the sentiment: "By humanitarianism I mean nothing more and nothing less than the study and practice of human principles—of compassion, love, gentleness, and universal benevolence" (Salt 1891, 3).

HUMANITARIANISM AND LIBERAL SOCIETY

The study therefore analyzes the relationship between humanitarianism and the emergence of liberal society, with its distinctive features of capitalism (the market) and democracy (civic equality and citizenship). That humanitarianism is associated with the rise of liberal society is undoubted. But we must press beyond the purported inconsistency between liberal humanitarianism and the equally undoubted individualism and public indifference of liberal society. The sense of inconsistency between these two images of liberal democracy as a moral system is due in part to sentimentalism and nostalgia (for example, Nisbet 1961; Tönnies 1887) and in part to an image of liberal society as pervasively oppressive (for example, Foucault 1977). Both approaches suffer from the presentist assumption that moral sentiments like compassion are "more" or "less" present in contemporary society. The study of specific cases has not sufficiently been informed by a historical sense of transformations in the meaning of compassion.

Among modern sociologists and historians of civil society critical of this liberal vision, doubts about such a focus of morality have arisen. This critical vision is influenced by the teachings of Nietzsche, Freud, and Marx, each emphasizing ulterior motives and material interests underlying all "lofty" moral ideals. Under the new political and social freedoms that market society and democracy have brought upon modern society lurk new constraints. Modern society diminishes community and solidarity. Altruism and compassion are expressions of the "will to power," "libidinal instincts," or "class control," or a mixture of these. Critics have interpreted "public compassion" and "social control" as mechanisms of class control and state power (Donzelot 1979; Katz 1986). The emphasis in these approaches is on conflict rather than on harmony, and on control from above rather than on a moral community based on self-control and active and mutually influencing agents. Furthermore, these approaches have drawn attention to the material interests underlying moral reform and accompanying ideals like compassion.

Michel Foucault (1965, 1977), in his earlier works, is among the most influential of these writers. Here, the history of reform over the last centuries is the desire of those in power to control and discipline society. Foucault gives little credit to Enlightenment humanitarianism. In humanitarian reforms he sees an attempt to put people into sophisticated prisons of disciplining technologies. Modern human sciences have taken over the role of Christianity in disciplining the body.

Recent studies in the morality of modern society (especially Bauman 1989, 1993, 1995) argue that distance between people prevents all moral relations between them. The invisible other is turned into a morally lost other. There exist no moral relations between strangers. Bauman suggests instead "a-sociological" moral relations. These are relations that are based on a Levinasian "unconditional responsibility for the other" (see also Lash 1996).

One purpose of this book is not only to investigate the question of whether public compassion is only the ideology of social control—as most contemporary sociological approaches seem to suggest—or whether public compassion is part of a new moral self-perception. With that in mind, this study tries to reconstruct compassion as part of the cultural value system of modernity, seeing how it can be grounded in real-life experiences of social individual actors.

DEMOCRACY AND THE MARKET

To this point, two broad interpretations of the emergence and rise of public compassion have been developed. The democratization perspective suggests that with the lessening of profoundly categorical and corporate social distinctions, compassion becomes more extensive. A second perspective is linked to the emergence of market society. In this perspective, the market itself can be understood to extend the public scope of compassion. By defining a universal field of others with whom contracts and exchanges can be made, market perspectives extend the sphere of moral concern as well, however unintentionally.

In both perspectives, with the onset of civil society the nature and sentiment of compassion changed. As a "natural" moral sentiment, public compassion involves a revolution in sensibility. This shift in sensibilities also meant a new relationship to pain. Pain was considered an evil of the past, and humanitarian efforts in every field of reform were mostly concerned with the abolition of pain. Public compassion was initially the fight against cruelty, understood as the unjustifiable affliction of pain. Modern humanitarianism protests against such suffering and pain. In its philanthropic version, it tried to establish bonds of compassion among social groups and classes.

Public compassion must be distinguished from earlier models of compassion like religious charity, as well as later models like the bureaucratic welfare state. When humanitarian compassion is organized in pressure groups aiming at legislative measures to cure or prevent suffering, as semigovernmental institutions, or as political parties with this aim, we speak of public compassion (Brinton 1937). Modern humanitarian movements arose in the eighteenth and nineteenth centuries. Movements to abolish slavery and cruelty to prisoners, animals, and children and to reform factories, sanitation, and prisons were organized during that time and continue today.

Humanitarian movements delegitimized earlier values and practices as morally reprehensible. In the rhetoric of humanitarian reform, these older practices were often redefined as cruel. Cruelty became understood as the infliction of suffering without the old justifications for it, and compassion in organized form a public response to this evil. For example, public executions, torture, and slavery came under moral scrutiny. Why, then, did humanitarian movements appear during that time in most countries of the West?

CAPITALISM AND COMPASSION

Since these humanitarian movements arose at much the same time that the market displaced earlier forms of economic organization, we must inquire into the relationship between humanitarian sensibilities and the emergence of market society. Could it be the case that there is a connection between market society and capitalism, and the rise of humanitarian sensibilities (Haskell 1985)?

If market behavior consists of the relentless pursuit of profit, a capitalist "moral cosmology" is impossible to deduce. Some have argued that the market depletes the moral legacy that it inherits. For instance, Joseph Schumpeter (1942) and Fred Hirsch (1976) hold that a social morality motivating concern about others is a legacy of the precapitalist and preindustrial past. Schumpeter believes that capitalism, while a success as an economic system, will not avoid decline since it cannot produce a new code of morality without destroying that which it has inherited. There is for him a tragic "contradiction" between the means necessary for capitalism's economic performance and those required for its cultural legitimization. In such views public compassion and humanitarian movements are incompatible with the self-interested rationality of market society, but are "carry-over" effects from precapitalist eras or noneconomic factors constraining the market.

Other critics of market society united by their sentimental longing for *gemeinschaftliche* solidarity (such as the young, romantic Marx and Ferdinand Tönnies) have considered capitalism to lack ethical principles. The world of capitalism is devoid of tender feelings toward strangers, informed solely by self-interest, cold and callous toward fellow human beings, seeing them only as instruments to one's own ends. In a typical statement the romantic Marx remarked:

> The bourgeoisie, wherever it has got the upper hand, has put an end to all feudal, patriarchal, idyllic relations. It has *pitilessly* torn asunder the motley feudal ties that bound man to his "natural superiors," and has left remaining no other nexus between man and man than naked self-interest, than callous "cash payment." It has drowned the most heavenly ecstasies of religious fervor, of chivalrous enthusiasm, of philistine sentimentalism, in the icy water of egotistical calculation. It has resolved personal worth into exchange value, and in place of the numberless indefeasible chartered freedoms, has set up that single, unconscionable freedom—Free Trade. (Marx 1972, 475, my emphasis)

This statement expresses sensibilities representative of both conservative and romantic versions of the decline of community and the dominance of calculative self-interest as crucial to the loss of fellow feeling and compassion. Ferdinand Tönnies regarded the change from sacred–communal ideas to secular–associational ones as essential (Tönnies 1887; Nisbet 1966). The essence of market society is rationality and calculation. In this system, everybody is isolated, and no morality is possible. Echoing these thoughts, the interwar poet and critic Christopher Caudwell claimed that:

> As . . . [commodity] relations produced industrial capitalism and the modern bourgeois State, it sucked the tenderness out of all social relations. . . . Love and economic relations have gathered at two opposite poles. (quoted in Silver 1990b, 1475)

Adorno and Horkheimer also claim that the essence of "compassion" is nothing other than the narcissistic desires of an exploitative bourgeoisie to feel good about itself (Horkheimer and Adorno 1944, 93). These ideas leave no room for the possibilities that modern society can develop any sense of moral responsibility. It also collapses market society into mere profit making. However, market behavior is not only about profit making. Does market society civilize behavior as, among others, Elias (1978) and Hirschman (1982) have argued? Is there a form of compassion distinctive to market society, a bond among members of civil society that shapes encounters with the sufferings of others? Are the market and its behaviors and sensibilities necessarily detrimental to the emergence of public compassion?

THE HISTORICAL VICISSITUDES OF COMPASSION

Contrary to clichés of *Gesellschaft* perspectives as exemplified by Tönnies and others, market society might extend the scope of public compassion. By defining a universal field of others with whom contracts and exchanges can be made, market perspectives also extend the sphere of moral concern, however unintentionally (for example, Gatrell 1994; Haskell 1985; Silver 1990b). To demonstrate that public compassion and humanitarian sensibilities are indeed part of the moral universe of market society and capitalism, it is necessary to show that these historically specific forms of compassion differ from earlier ones. Hannah Arendt has remarked:

> History tells us that it is by no means a matter of course for the spectacle of misery to move men to pity; even during the long centuries when the Christian religion of mercy determined moral standards of Western civilization, compassion operated outside the political realm and frequently outside the established hierarchy of the Church. (Arendt 1963, 65)

Arendt's agenda is not to study the vicissitudes of compassion, but rather to demonstrate the inadequacy of compassion as a political principle and to argue that compassion and virtue are not necessarily identical (Canovan 1992). Indeed, in the medieval period, compassion did not sustain organized helping. The demand to help others was based on the Christian principle of *agape*. (See Nygren 1938 for an influential Lutheran interpretation of *agape*.) A classical statement of Christian agape is the thirteenth chapter of Paul's First Letter to the Corinthians (where *agape* is translated as "love"):

> Love is patient and kind; love is not jealous or boastful, it is not arrogant or rude. Love does not insist on its own way; it is not irritable or resentful; it does not rejoice at wrong, but rejoices in the right. Love bears all things, hopes all things, endures all things. Love never ends. (1 Cor. 13)

Agape is spontaneous, unconditional, and unmotivated, and according to Nygren (1938) is indifferent to the value of the one who is loved. Fellowship with God is governed by love, not by law. God's attitude to humanity is not characterized by *justitia distributiva* but by agape, not by retributive righteousness but by freely giving and forgiving love (Nygren, 70). Even the demand to "love thy neighbor as thyself" is not comparable to public compassion or the secular vision of "love of mankind." The Christian's love of neighbor is a manifestation of God's *agape*, in which both believer and neighbor are occasions of its expression. Christian doctrine demanded charity in the form of feeding the hungry, the alleviation of pain, and the kindly treatment of strangers. However, *agape* did not imply a political or moral principle (Niebuhr 1956). Even though there were innumerable attempts to alleviate suffering, the idea that suffering in itself was wrong did not play a part in Christianity's notion of transcendental and universal love.

Benjamin Nelson (1949), in his study of moral evolution concerning the transition from "brotherhood" to "otherhood," observed the "lowering of the moral standard" of *caritas* among theologians and moralists of the seventeenth and eighteenth centuries. Thus, according to Nelson, William Paley, in *Principles of Moral and Political Philosophy* (1785), redefines charity:

> I use the term Charity neither in the common sense of bounty to the poor, nor in St. Paul's sense of benevolence to all mankind: but I apply it at present, in a sense more commodious to my purpose, to signify promoting the happiness of our inferiors. (Nelson 1949, 162–63)

With the idea of "promoting the happiness of our inferiors" we move from Christian doctrine to Christian ethics, a semisecularized concept. While the language of many reformers remains religious, it is transformed by secularization. Together with the love of self emerges a secular concept of happiness. So long as love of self was considered a turning away from God and as sin, the human demand for happiness could only be realized in a theological context, as selfless love of God or as salvation. A morally justified self-love seeks its realization in a "natural" striving for happiness, emancipated from theological demands and expressing itself as "moral sentiment." Furthermore, the regulation of social and political life, the *civitas terrena*, was seen as the result of fundamental guilt and sin caused by the Fall. Love as God's attribute was part of the *civitas dei*. These two worlds were aptly symbolized by the two ideal heroes of the medieval Christian world, knight and saint.

Medieval charity does not, therefore, express universal sympathy and a striving for human happiness. It differs from modern humanitarianism, based on public compassion. It alleviated suffering, but did not imagine the possibility of ending it. Indeed, given the Fall and humanity's sinful nature, it presupposed the inevitability and the justice of suffering in this world. Therefore "Love of mankind" as a principle of the Enlightenment on which public compassion is based has to be distinguished from "neighborly love" (Fuerth 1933; Levie 1975). The motive for "neighborly love" and charity was God's command. On the other hand, modern humanitarianism is directed toward humanity's material and ethical existence.

Public compassion has a theoretical source and origin not in divine will and agape, but in an abstract and rational idea of humanity. The common good replaces salvation. This sense of shared humanity implies an equality if not of status then of moral claim. Public compassion demands the performance of beneficent actions involving a certain kind of imaginative power to reconstruct others' conditions, an act of empathy implying a fundamental equality in human experience and moral status. In the history of ideas about moral conduct, compassion in premodern times did not play a major role. The classical moral traditions subordinated compassion to considerations of reason and prudence, whereas religious tradition distinguished very clearly between goodness in man and the goodness of God. Neither in antiquity nor in the Middle Ages has the "man of feeling" ever been a popular type (Crane 1934; Campbell 1987). This does not mean that there is a radical disjunction between agape and modern compassion. However, as the following section will show, a change in emphasis is apparent.

THE LATITUDINARIANS

The origins of this new doctrine do not lie, as generally assumed, in the moral theorists of the eighteenth century, such as those of the Scottish Enlightenment, but can be traced to numerous Anglican divines of the Latitudinarian tradition in England between 1660 and 1725. Latitudinarian preachers sought to combat Puritan pessimism about human nature, and Hobbesian egoism, elevating universal benevolence as a prime religious virtue. For these thinkers charity was extremely important, but as generalized kindness rather than as *agape dei*. They rejected the Stoic notion that although the good man must relieve the distress of others, he must not allow himself to be emotionally affected by their misfortunes. Equally, they rejected Hobbes's pessimistic picture of natural man and Hobbes's claim in *Leviathan* that without strong authority the natural passions lead to the "warre of all against all." The theorists of benevolence claimed that human beings are naturally disposed to live together in mutually helpful ways and are capable of moral self-regulation. Furthermore, they claimed that there was no conflict between individual and social welfare. "The man of feeling" became a new moral hero. Four principal aspects of latitudinarian ethical thinking are important to note here: virtue as universal benevolence; benevolence as feeling; benevolent feelings as "natural"; and "self-approving joy" (Crane 1934). In their sermons, which attacked Puritan and Catholic ideas, especially those of predestination and men's wicked nature, they emphasized that the prosperous benefited because they worked, and success in this world as well as in the next rested not with predestination but with acts of individual will (Halttunen 1995; Jacob 1976; Schlatter 1940).

In many respects, the social ideas of the Latitudinarian preachers of the seventeenth century resembled those of the later Scottish Enlightenment. They were Christian humanists, believing that self-interest would become enlightened and that private interest would flourish in the service of public interest. In their sermons, they addressed themselves primarily to the public actions of the Christian; they seldom discussed inner spirituality. According to Jacob (1976), the most historically significant contribution of the Latitudinarians lay with their ability to synthesize the operations of a market society and the workings of nature in such a way as to render market society natural—and this precisely at a time when modern and capitalist forms of economic life and social relations were gaining ascendancy. They proposed a Christianized capitalism, an ethic for self-interest resting upon the providential order in the political and natural worlds. They also qualified the concept of charity: they recognized it, of course, as a primary Christian virtue, but also believed that those who voluntarily chose poverty out of laziness deserved to starve or be put in workhouses. Charity should only be given to the deserving poor. With this notion they apparently started the long debate on the distinction between the "deserving" and "undeserving" poor, a distinction unknown to the theological concept of agape.

The elevation of the "tender passions" as virtues had, therefore, a moral as well as a theological context. In its moral context, "natural compassion" is an autonomous mechanism of human nature, a concern of secularized Enlightenment philosophy. In theology the questions were about the nature of God: are the passions of God in any way comparable to those of men? For humanitarian thinkers nothing was more absurd than the idea that goodness in man is not the same as goodness in God. This new teaching conflicted with the dogma of original sin, as well as with the orthodox doctrine of hell, which perceived no contradiction between God's agape and everyday cruelties or the miseries of those damned in the life thereafter. So, although coined in religious language, it presents a secularized form of the older Christian doctrines.

THE SCOTTISH ENLIGHTENMENT

Eighteenth-century British theorists of civil society like Shaftesbury, Butler, Hutchenson, Hume, and Smith developed a theory of "moral sense," addressing the problem of sympathy and compassion. Sympathy is a weak form of compassion. While compassion knows few limits, sympathy is conditional on others' appropriate behavior. They considered "natural compassion" descriptive of human nature as well as normative (Hume 1751; Smith 1759). Human beings both have, and ought to have, fellow feelings for others. As an automatic mechanism for the common good, sympathy is thus seen to lie in the very nature of civil society. Adam Smith's *Theory of Moral Sentiments* begins by ascribing the source of concern for others in human nature:

How selfish soever man may be supposed, there are evidently some principles in his nature, which interest him in the fortune of others, and render their happiness necessary to him, though he derives nothing from it except the pleasure of seeing it. Of this kind is pity or compassion, the emotion which we feel for the misery of others, when we either see it, or are made to conceive it in a very lively manner. (Smith 1759, 9)

Smith assumes that "we often derive sorrow from the sorrow of others," continuing, that it is "a matter of fact too obvious to require any instances to prove it." This "natural" approach to understanding compassion is expressed by Hume in the observation that "It is needless to push our researches so far as to ask, why we have humanity or a fellow-feeling with others. It is sufficient, that this is experienced to be a principle in human nature" (Hume 1751, 43).

In this conception, imagination is key to compassion. Human beings are cruel because they cannot put themselves in the place of those who suffer. One has to imagine how one would feel in another's place. As Smith wrote:

as we have no immediate experience of what other men feel, we can form no idea of the manner in which they are affected, but by conceiving what we ourselves should feel in the like situation. Though our brother is upon the rack, as long as we ourselves are at our ease, our senses will never inform us of what he suffers. They never did, and never can, carry us beyond our own person, and it is by the imagination only that we can form any conception of what are his sensations. (Smith 1759, 9)

To experience "natural" compassion, we must rely on our own senses. Compassion in this ethical system takes individualism and one's own experience of suffering as points of departure. Emotional separateness and distance, essential to individualism, are constitutive of fellow feeling, as distinct from *agape* and *caritas*. Emotional separateness and distance, prevalent in market society, thus enable members of civil society to form a bond that shapes encounters with the suffering of others. Smith in particular emphasized the consistency between concern for the self and distance from others on the one hand, and the emergence of moral conduct on the other. Sympathy grows out of these separate experiences of individuals and is therefore consistent with market society. Smith emphasizes the self-love of humankind in what he calls commercial society. People who were previously indifferent to each other can enter now into contractual market exchanges (Silver 1990b). This kind of structural distance between individuals makes it possible to bring them together in a common public realm (Berry 1994; Boltanski 1993).

This sort of compassion is an unheroic quality, unlike the absolute goodness of saints. Self-love and compassion are intrinsically linked and coexist within individuals (Mizuta 1975). The problem these thinkers strove to solve was the relationship between self-interested individuals and benevolent or other-oriented moral conduct. This tension is particularly clear in Smith's two major works, *The Theory of Moral Sentiments* (1759) and *The Wealth of Nations* (1776). That the same author wrote on political economy and moral sentiments, on self-interest and sympathy, seemed to many an inconsistency, the so-called Das Adam Smith Problem (Oncken 1897). The apparent problem lies in the assumption that compassion and benevolence are inconsistent with market structures based on individual self-interest. However, compassion's dependence on imagination and the individual self is crucial for the emergence of moral sentiments. Here Smith broke with the dominant tradition in moral philosophy that regarded communality, not distance, as the key to fellow feeling (Agnew 1986). Smith's concern was with the interpersonal behavior of civil society. Compassion thus originated in the mutual inaccessibility of individuals. One of the consequences of this view of compassion as "benevolent sympathy" in nineteenth-century reform policy was that it became conditional on the "good" or "appropriate" behavior of those who "deserve" sympathy. As opposed to agape, which is unconditional and indifferent to the value of the one who is loved, compassion as "benevolent sympathy" in the liberal setting is very much conditional on its being deserved.

As opposed to Tönnies and others in his tradition, Smith proposed a *Gesellschaft* of compassionate people. In the new market society, suffering is recreated imaginatively in the minds of public spectators. The existence of "public imagination" is in itself, as Habermas (1962) has written, characteristic of market society. The public sphere is an arena for concerns important to all. The separation between private and public spheres is also characterized by the emergence of a new religious conscience and the realization that it is impossible to impose morality through the official creed of the state or the official church. Therefore, to experience compassion without transcending individualism, to imagine others' sufferings through a mechanism that informs us how we would suffer in the other's place, we experience compassion best with people most like ourselves (Radner 1979).

THE SENTIMENTALIZATION OF COMPASSION

The stoic qualities of Smith's eighteenth-century thought were increasingly sentimentalized during the end of the eighteenth and the course of the nineteenth centuries. A specific example of the sentimentalization of eighteenth-century vocabulary is the case of torture. Having removed torture from its specific place in the legal system and indicted it as a moral transgression, nineteenth-century thinkers widened its definition. The applicability of the term was broadened to all areas of human brutality. All oppressors tortured all oppressed. Terms like "animal torture," or "torture of women and children," became part of the standard moral vocabulary of nineteenth-century reform. Torture was identified with inhuman practices (Peters 1985).

Compassion played a formative role in the establishment of Western humanitarianism, and it was and still is presented as both normative and prescriptive. We are compassionate, and if we are not we ought to be. Only in a democratic setting can compassion be almost substitutive for representation. Public compassion is not only an individual manifestation of human conduct and care for others. Such episodes of human conduct occur everywhere and at all times. A sociology of public compassion addresses a social and collective pattern of conduct in which substantial numbers of people believe that to alleviate the sufferings, pains, and humiliations of others is the right thing to do.

COMPASSION AND THE SOCIOLOGY OF MORALS

This study of compassion is therefore also an exercise in the sociology of morals. An empirical and sociological study of morality has to be both descriptive and normative. It not only inquires about the social and historical conditions of its emergence, but seeks to answer the question of how moral sentiments can serve as a basis for a theory of social relations. What is clear from this short historical introduction is that compassion as moral sentiment has become not only a moral obligation but a learned practice. I will show this later in detail.

Liberal theory had to tackle the problem of moral obligations to others by asking, "Who is responsible for others if each individual in civil society is primarily concerned with his own well-being?" Was a new form of compassion possible given the assumption of self-interested individuals? Persons in modern civil society were transformed, routinely acquiring qualities previously regarded as divine. As I have shown, this understanding was far removed from revealed religious perceptions of compassion, which is based on God's compassion alone. ("Yet, he, being compassionate, forgave their iniquity, and did not destroy them; he restrained his anger often, and did not stir up all his wrath." [Ps., 78.38]) As a consequence, in precivil society there was no disparity between the principle of Christian love and the acceptance of suffering. Christian love was not meant to be a social principle. This understanding of moral obligation changed with the emergence of civil society.

However, there are not only postmodern reactions against compassion as with Bauman (1993), for example, but "bourgeois moral sentiments" are being attacked by the enemies of postmodernism as well. There is a neoconservative reaction against compassion (Himmelfarb 1991; Orwin 1980; for a neoliberal rejection of compassion as moral and political sentiment, see Kaus 1986). This new critique of compassion acknowledges its emotional and moral power. Gertrude Himmelfarb (1991, 5–6) distinguishes between two forms of compassion: "sentimental" and "unsentimental," the latter being "compassion properly understood." She defines "sentimental" compassion as an exercise in feeling good, rather than doing good, whereas "right" compassion seeks to do good according to the principles of prudence. However, the intellectual grounds for this distinction are shaky. They cannot be found in the original eighteenth-century teaching of compassion. These teachings rejected the classical and Stoical ideal of the separation between reason and sentiment, which lies behind the criticism of Himmelfarb. Hence, when Himmelfarb in her rejection of sentimental compassion argues that "to be truly humane, genuinely compassionate, was not to be selfless; it was only to be true to one's 'best self' and to the 'common good' that includes one's own good," she argues against a teaching of compassion that never existed: all teachers of compassion since Rousseau and Smith have agreed that the self is the starting point for sentiments of compassion. Himmelfarb has a different agenda. In her very suggestive historical analysis of late-Victorian political and moral reform in England, she wants to rehabilitate the often discredited Victorian reformers. Furthermore, she rejects the egalitarian tendencies of the modern welfare state, which separates morality from social policy.

In a similar vein, Clifford Orwin (1980)—a Straussian political theorist—in a very interesting historical and political analysis of compassion, rejects it as a guide for political conduct. Orwin argues that compassion implies caring without judging, and acting morally while refraining from enacting one's own morals. The experience of compassion betrays no rift between inclination and duty and has therefore no guiding sense of proportion.

Both writers, in their rejection of compassion, evoke Kant as a guide to moral conduct. Kant rejected compassion on the grounds that feelings, unlike reason, have no proportion. Kant argued that no emotionally governed activity can contribute to our assessment of this activity's being moral:

> To be beneficent, that is, to promote according to one's means the happiness of others in need, without hoping for something in return, is every man's duty. For every man who finds himself in need wishes to be helped by other men. But if he lets his maxim of being unwilling to assist others in turn when they are in need become public, that is, makes this a universal permissive law, then everyone would likewise deny him assistance when he himself is in need, or at least would be authorized to deny it. Hence the maxim of self-interest would conflict with itself if it were made a universal law, that is contrary to duty. Consequently the maxim of common interest, of beneficence toward those in need, is a universal duty of men, just because they are to be considered fellow men, that is rational beings with needs, united by nature in one dwelling place so that they can help each other. (Kant 1991, 247)

It is on these Kantian grounds that compassion is rejected by the critics of modern liberal politics, identifying it with an overindulgence in feelings. Compassion based on feeling cannot provide a principle when these compassionate feelings have to stop. As Kaus (1986) argues in this Kantian mode, "common interest should serve as an anti-pode to compassion" (18). This ethical universalism and its demand for justice has been taken over from Christianity. The Christian idea of moral perfection is to treat everyone as a fellow sinner and member of the community of faith. This aspect of Christian ethical universality is particularly expressed in Luke 10.29 in the parable of the "Good Samaritan." Jesus tells this story in answer to the question "And who is my neighbor?"—the answer being: everyone in need and not only your immediate neighbor. (For a suggestive discussion on this point, see Rorty 1989, 192ff).

Kant looked for a basis of moral obligation that was not contingent on sentiment and historical particularities, the consequence of which was that the identification with other people's suffering, the basis of compassion, was to become suspect as the basis of morality.

Moral theories taking duties or fundamental rights as a guidepost for moral conduct focus almost exclusively on the individual. There has been increasing criticism of such individual-based moral theories from a group of social philosophers who seek to move the ethical debate closer to the concerns of sociologists. They can be loosely called *communitarians*. This perspective, expressed in particular by Alasdair MacIntyre's *After Virtue* (1984), William Sullivan's *Reconstructing Public Philosophy* (1982), and Amitai Etzioni's *The Spirit of Community* (1994), judges moral actions on their fit with the contingent traditions of the community rather than in terms of universal principles. MacIntyre, especially, tries to move the debate on moral obligations closer to a historical understanding of contingency:

> One reason why claims about goods necessary for rational agency are so different from claims to the possession of rights is that the latter in fact presuppose, as the former do not, the existence of a socially established set of rules. Such sets of rules only come into existence at particular historical periods under particular social circumstances. (MacIntyre 1984, 62)

Sullivan (1982) shares MacIntyre's criticism of universal moral principles. Both thinkers take Aristotle as their guide for a correct moral and political philosophy and a restoration of civic culture:

> A civic culture is necessarily defined by its two poles: it is aiming at universal sympathy, an ideal enunciated by the Stoics and given powerful expression in Christian natural law teaching; yet, civic culture is grounded and rooted in historical circumstances of its place of origin and the particular conditions of life in which it comes to grow. (Sullivan 1982, 170)

People's commitments must, therefore, be to the community, to the shared life, to civic life.

These modern debates about the moral worth of compassion are as old as ethical theory itself. Ancient philosophers like Plato and Aristotle rejected compassion as the basis of moral obligations because it carried the danger of overwhelming us with emotions, a sentiment identified with "femaleness" and detrimental to the ancients' concern with timeless justice as the basis of moral virtue.

Compassion and pity were seen as the loss of moral autonomy and of self-control. Moral obligations in this perspective should be directed from above through tight political control. These sentiments were and are echoed in conservative thought, classical and modern.

This dilemma is also addressed by communitarianism. The communitarians challenge individual-based ethical theories on both moral and sociological grounds. Sociologically, they recognize the limits of nomadic individualism and propose a theory of individualism that perceives no possibility of the individual as an abstract concept outside the social realm. For the communitarians, the phenomenon of individualism is not seen against social structure, but as constituted by social structure. Morally and historically, they attempt to reclaim the Aristotelian tradition of civic virtue.

In terms of the moral debate, communitarians fear the destructive influence of Nietzsche and his followers in the social sciences. To avoid Nietzsche, they return to Aristotle. Nietzsche, of course, is the inspiration for the deconstructionist and postmodern criticism of the possibility of moral foundations in general (Bauman 1995; Harvey 1989; Turner 1990). Nietzsche rejected the Enlightenment deliberations on civilization, reason, and universality and proposed to substitute for them a destructive creativity based on the will to power and the desire to act. All formulations of moral conduct are attempts by the weak to curb the power of the strong. Morality can only be what the will creates (see also Maffesoli 1995 with his notion of an "aesthetic ethics" in this connection). Nietzsche was also one of the strongest critics of compassion. He considered it (in a way similar to Kant, whose philosophy he otherwise rejected) as a contagious disease, a loss of autonomy and self-control (Cartwright 1984). For Nietzsche, compassion and love are but expressions of resentment, bitterness, and hatred of the lower classes of society for their superiors. Love and compassion are nothing but instrumental means to achieve societal goals. But even Nietzsche had to recognize that these sentiments had to occur in a democratic society with egalitarian values. For Nietzsche, these sentiments were a logical and historical development from Christian concepts of love. However, here Nietzsche confuses Christian *agape* with a generalized and universal love of mankind characteristic for modern society. Modern humanitarianism and *agape*, even though sharing common characteristics, are structurally and historically different, as are the principles of the "salvation of souls" and the "common good" (Scheler 1924). Scheler agrees with the analysis put forward here that modern humanitarianism emerged in democratic societies, but he perceives it as moral decadence from the more spiritual aspects of *agape*.

TOWARD A POLITICAL SOCIOLOGY OF MORALITY

Where do these debates, centered around questions of moral relativism versus moral absolutism, duty versus inclination, reason versus sentiment, leave the sociologist interested in the sociology of moral conduct? Does one have to take the side of the deconstructionist and postmodernist and other assaults on so-called foundationalism in order to accept that human morality is historically contingent and a product of social relations? Or does one have to take the side of communitarian foundationalism in order to reject approaches that consider morality only as tools in power struggles?

Compassion is also understood as a force against the market. The theme occurs in one of the very few contemporary pleas for a moral sociology, Alan Wolfe's *Whose Keeper?* (1989). His is a "social construction" of morality approach achieved through the interaction of morally conscious beings: "Against the penetration of the market into the realm of civil society, as has occurred in the United States, should be balanced the capacity of people to treat one another out of compassion and generosity" (235). However, since Wolfe takes as his market model the "economic man" concept of the Chicago School, he overlooks that this capacity to treat one another with compassion and generosity has also been an unintended consequence of the market itself. Interaction in civil society without embeddedness in the market or the modern nation-state is an impossible abstraction, since both the market and the modern state make possible interaction in civil society. Citizens in modern states are dependent upon the services and provisions organized by the state. As modern market societies make it impossible for individuals to be autarkic, reliance on a civil society, disembedded from market and state, as a guarantor of moral obligations is dubious. Others take a more authoritarian approach and demand to "remoralize" citizens' obligation to the state (Mead 1986).

My study on the emergence of public compassion is an attempt to provide an alternative to these views by reconstructing the language of compassion from bourgeois discourse itself. We need to try to transcend idealistic or materialist theories concerning the origin of humanitarianism and maintain both aspects at the same time (see also Haskell 1985). There is indeed historical contingency with regard to the emergence of humanitarian sentiments, including moral compassion. There are sociological forms of understanding that recognize the social origin of moral sentiments without reducing them to epiphenomena or ideological superstructures of the will to power or attempts by the ruling elements of society to control the masses or curb unrest. Moral compassion is not merely epiphenomenal, emerging in a specific historical and social context, namely through the emergence of capitalism. The market, through its universal features, allows people participating in it to enter—independent of their will—into universal moral relationships. The market expands the horizons of people's moral responsibility, formerly limited by exclusivistic bonds of memberships in corporate groups. Public compassion thus emerges from market relationships.

There is another feature of capitalist society partly responsible for this, namely democracy. We have suggested that with the lessening of profoundly categorical and corporate social distinctions, compassion becomes more extensive. The capacity to identify with others, and in particular with others' pain, is promoted by the profound belief that others are similar to us. This identification is based on civic equality. Tocqueville observed the capacity in America to identify with others and extend the circle of compassion to everybody. In democracy, everybody is formally in the same moral arena. He attributed this to the condition of political equality, which made this moral state possible (Tocqueville 1840; see also Beck [1997a, 333–47], who talks about "the end of ontological differences" as a major point in Tocqueville's thought).

It was Émile Durkheim who tried both to systematize Tocqueville's observation and to put it into a coherent social theory and a sociology of morals and moral sociology at the same time. For Durkheim, moral ideas reflect social boundaries and in democracy these boundaries are widest: with the extension of mutual interdependency through an elaborate system of the division of labor, the moral sense expands and becomes more abstract and universal, the typical features of capitalist-market societies. Durkheim took some of his cues not only from Tocqueville, but also from the German philosopher Arthur Schopenhauer. Schopenhauer wrote in 1840 an essay called "On the Basis of Morality," in which he severely criticized Kant for his account of duty-based ethics. Schopenhauer held that compassion is the mainspring of morality and also suggested that it should be studied empirically, a project Durkheim tried to undertake (see Mestrovic 1993, 1997) on Schopenhauer, but also on a different approach to these questions. Durkheim's attempted project was to create a secular rational ethic. However, diverting from philosophical debates concerning the nature of morality, Durkheim's sociology of morals tries to start from moral facts, not from moral duties:

> There is between men an internal bond, which manifests itself in affections, sympathy, language, civil society, and is yet something more profound than all that, hidden in the recesses of the human essence. . . . Men, bound by a community of essence cannot say "I am indifferent to what concerns others." But whatever this solidarity may be, whatever its nature and its origins, it can only be presented as a fact, with no basis for presenting it as a duty. (Durkheim 1964, 413–14)

This quotation is from the preface to the first edition of *The Division of Labor* (orig. pub. 1893). The preface is an argument against Kantian and utilitarian ideas of morality, trying instead to present an outline for an empirical sociology of moral values (Hall 1987; Mestrovic 1988).

Durkheim's question was: What holds people together in an age of individualism? His answer was that the division of labor is not only a law of history but also the only basis of the ethical and social life. Even more, the division of labor is a source of ethical life. Durkheim recognizes that moral rules are only moral in relation to certain social and historical conditions; and since the division of labor becomes for Durkheim the chief source of social solidarity, it becomes at the same time the foundation of moral order. This, of course, defines Durkheim as a moral relativist, but whereas in philosophy, theories of moral obligation do not depend on consensus, in sociology they do. With his empirical sociology of morals, Durkheim tries to avoid both under- and oversocialized conceptions of humanity. He takes both agency and social determinism into account (see also Cladis 1993). Against the Kantian tradition, Durkheim thinks that justice in a modern democratic society begins with our emotional engagement in the world. Against the utilitarian tradition that finds humans equally capable of feeling pain and pleasure, with the pleasures of benevolence being the basis of moral sentiments, Durkheim thought with the rational philosophers that cruelty and suffering were out of place in an ordered universe. In his sociology of morals, rationalism and utilitarianism are interwoven, as he so powerfully suggests in his preface to the first edition of *The Division of Labor.* Durkheim shows that both duty and the pursuit of the "good" are products of social interaction in specific social and historical circumstances. His was an attempt to save the moral dimension of sociology by referring back to eighteenth-century formulations of natural sympathy and compassion (see also Seligman 1992). I think the important thing about Durkheim is the idea of liberalism as a religion—as a set of values that animates every modern state and that people believe in unconditionally, the same way they believe in religion. These values—democracy; individual rights; justice; equality before the law; compassion in our case—are simply true for believers in the creed. Once they are embodied in institutions, in habitus, in interpretations, then societies will continue to turn out believers. This will also point to why some societies are "more" compassionate than others. There are "God-given rights," and what is meant by that is that one does not ask preachers about them, but that those rights are written in democratic, liberal, Christian hearts, and that they must have been written there by God. This is my idea of liberalism as a moral force. We have to understand it as a religion, as something to be identified with the abolition of cruelty, which is different from secularized Christianity.

Against the Kantian critics of compassion like Himmelfarb (1991) and Orwin (1980), it can be shown that emotions are indeed rational, purposeful actions that fall into the realm of responsibility (Peters 1973; Rorty 1982). Or as Tocqueville recognized more than 150 years ago:

> In aristocratic ages each man is always bound by close ties to many of his fellow citizens so that he cannot be attacked without the others coming to his help. In times of equality each man is naturally isolated. He can call on no hereditary friends for help nor any class whose sympathy for him is assured. . . . Nowadays an oppressed citizen has only one means of defense: he can appeal to the nation as a whole, and if it is deaf, to humanity at large. (Tocqueville 1969, 697)

Is compassion at all possible in a society of individuals? I will try to argue in this book against the rather commonsense view found in the social sciences that treats morality from a stance of skepticism, cynicism, even indifference. If at all, compassion is treated as epiphenomenal, an ideological superstructure, an objectivating practice, or serving to carry out symbolic violence. As useful as these approaches are to open our eyes to "hidden motives," they close them at the same time to a tradition within modernity that stimulates this specific cultural value. Compassion and individuality do not have to contradict each other, as many argue. This was clearly shown, at least in ideal terms, in the theoretical writings of the Scottish Enlightenment. What does this mean for today's everyday life, more than two hundred years after the Scots wrote their books? Wuthrow (1991) has empirically demonstrated the connection between acts of compassion and individuality for the United States. We may speak of a phenomenon that can be called "altruistic individualism" (Beck 1997a, 1997b) and that might be part of what Ulrich Beck also calls "Second Modernity." This is a modernity that allows for seemingly contradictory features (like altruism and individualism) to exist together. Altruistic individualism needs a "modular" man or woman (Gellner 1994), a person who can be moral without needing a moral society, a person who can be moral in the morning and be an individualist in the afternoon. In short, a person living in civil society.

Compassion can be rational if we can move from the recognition of another's weakness, and the role it plays in his or her distress, to the realization that we, too, are vulnerable, and consequently not immune to misfortune (Snow 1991). And yet, as Tocqueville and Durkheim have shown, this ability to identify with others is strengthened by the perception that we are indeed similar to them. Democratic civil society, therefore, includes a self-regarding concern with one's own weaknesses and potential liability to misfortune. Democratic compassion, therefore, does not require us to identify with a common set of values and social ends. But it does secure conditions in which others as moral equals are candidates for compassionate concern. As such, it is highly relevant that social scientists start to reconstruct the moral language of modernity itself. (See Gellner's [1992] suggestion of taking a stance with regard to what he calls "Rationalist Fundamentalism.") Such an attempt is able to cut through the stalemate of the moral debate between postmodernists who either deny the existence of a moral subject at all, or even try to ground morality without society, and those who attempt to ground the moral subject in contingent communities that lose the moral universalism that was part of the promise of modernity. In the next step, I will reconstruct how this moral sentiment developed historically and how it was framed around the question of pain and the fight against it. I will concentrate mainly on the United States and England (also because they are considered model "capitalist" societies) as the carriers of these moral sentiments.

Chapter 2

Pain and Compassion

Compassion is about pain, about sensing other people's pain, about understanding pain, about trying to do something about it. This was not always the case. Therefore, this chapter will analyze the relationship between an assumed increased sensitivity to physical pain and the emergence of liberal society, with its distinctive features of capitalism (the market) and democracy (civic equality and citizenship). Sociological research in the problem of pain has mainly been informed by Mark Zbrowski's book *People in Pain* (1969), a study in the social and cultural aspects of the pain experience. He found that ethnic groups offered their members patterns of attitudes and reactions to pain that were peculiar to the respective group. However, his study was characterized by cultural stereotypes, which remained ahistorical and unchanging (Kleinman et al. 1992, 2). On the other hand, Zbrowski's study opened an opportunity to develop a sociology of pain through further research and theory construction (Encandela 1993). The question to be asked is how and to what extent society and culture modify and shape the behavior of the person in pain as well as the perception of pain. Is there a limited set of historical and sociological categories that people draw on to describe pain, and what are the available models of pain in a specific culture? The study of specific cases of dealing with pain has not sufficiently been informed by a historical sense of transformations in its meaning (see also Morris 1991), and its connection to compassion has often been hidden from plain view.

With the onset of civil society the nature and sentiment of people's relationship to pain changed. This involved a revolution in sensibility. It contained a new aversion to pain, to be avoided at all cost. Pain was considered evil and happiness the absence of pain. Humanitarian efforts in every field of reform during the last two centuries have been mostly concerned with the abolition of pain. These efforts were composed initially of the fight against cruelty, understood as the unjustifiable infliction of pain. Modern humanitarianism protests against such suffering and pain. In its philanthropic version, it tried to establish bonds of compassion among social groups and classes. People's relationship to pain and suffering changes as moral concepts concerning these issues change. With the change of these moral concepts, social life changes as well. The study of the delegitimation of cruelty and the struggle against senseless pain and suffering can therefore demonstrate empirically how moral concepts and social life are intertwined without falling into one-sided causal determinism. The changing language of cruelty is not only a cultural artifact representing underlying interests, but has to be understood as constituting these interests at the same time. Since a sociological study of the transformation of the valuation of pain cannot be constructed through the reconstruction of the subjective experience of suffering, we will restrict ourselves to organized reactions against others' pain.

CRUELTY AND SOCIETY

The sociological literature on the transformation of social behavior (including the responsiveness to pain) is suggestive and provides large-scale interpretations regarding the emergence of bourgeois virtues such as revulsion against pain. Weber's idea of rationalization, Elias's "civilization process," and Oestreich's emergence of social discipline offer settings for the techniques of intervention into the lives of citizens and of the fight against cruelty. Oestreich (1969), concerned with state formation in early modern Europe, stressed the mix between "policing and pedagogy," in which the citizen had to adjust to the claim for order made by the state; Elias (1978) formulated a picture of the "civilizing process" in which growing social complexity and the increasing monopoly of violence by the state were mirrored in the standards of behavior of individuals through control of affect, cleanliness, and the increasing sense of shame. Weber was interested in how the rationalization processes affected individuals, including the methodic–rational way of life that excludes cruel excess (Weber 1968). These studies provide a "big picture" in which cruelty became an "anti-ideal" to be fought.

Liberalism, more than other political and social theory, tried to come to terms with people's heightened sensitivity to pain (see also Wolin 1960, 324ff). It will be argued here that pain has become one way of symbolic exchange in the modern world. Heightened sensitivity to pain gains social significance when society moves from a system of stratified relations into functional relations, as in the transition from the feudal to the market society. It will therefore be argued that democracy and the market cause heightened sensitivity to pain. I think that if we understand how the experience of pain is decisively shaped or modified in these specific historical and social settings, we can also understand how compassion operates under those circumstances. I will therefore explore the historical, cultural, and psychosocial construction of pain.

In precivil society, the imagination of suffering could not cross social boundaries as in democratic society, where the distance between formally and legally equal citizens is the same for all. At least in this liberal vision, humanitarianism is part of a larger middle-class project based on the ideals of eliminating pain and the desire to reduce cruelty. In earlier centuries there was no escape from pain. People took it as part of their lives or as punishment for their sins. Suffering pain might be considered a sign of blessedness. However, with the old theodicies gone, there was no blessedness in suffering pain. Pain could be mastered and should be avoided. It became an evil.

Huizinga demonstrated the medieval acceptance of violence in his classic study of 1924. Recent research has confirmed his view (Delumeau 1978; Hanawalt 1976; Muchembled 1989; Rouche 1987). To the medieval world, violence was a part of God's plan. Suffering, insecurity, violence were everyday occurrences. There was no cure for suffering, while eighteenth- and nineteenth-century reformers considered suffering as subject to remedy. Before the advent of this perspective, saints are the prototypical Christian heroes; their struggle is with evil and their victory is God's. The life of saints manifests *imitatio dei* and *agape dei.* Though modern reformers may have taken medieval saints like Francis of Assisi as models, the two were deeply different. The love Francis preached and practiced was hardly the same as the modern humanitarian's desire for universal happiness on this earth. Unlike the eighteenth-century reformers, medieval saints accepted the "cruelties" of medieval life.

But the taste for, and acceptance of, conduct later called "cruel" was not limited to the warrior class. As Norbert Elias and Barbara Hanawalt have shown, the life of burghers was also permeated by continued violence. Robbery, fighting, pillage, family feuds played an important part among town dwellers and peasants, as among the warrior classes. Burglars casually and sadistically killed their victims; neighbors beat each other to death over the value of a candle; apprentices killed little boys for befouling the streets. Judicial "cruelty" was common.

Torture and executions were enjoyed by spectators, who welcomed these spectacles of suffering (Spierenburg 1984). However, torture and inflicted pain were not understood as "cruel" in the modern sense. The modern concept of "cruelty" as characteristic of the penal system of premodern times was deemed as such by Enlightenment thinkers (Dülmen 1985). The purpose of the premodern penal system was not to reform the criminal offender, but to reestablish the moral order by inflicting physical suffering on transgressors. Torture was part of the legal procedure in the majority of European states. Especially in legal systems, which relied on confessions as proof of guilt, torture was a means to provide confessions (Langbein 1977). From the second half of the thirteenth century to the end of the eighteenth century torture was precise, limited, and highly regulated. The law represented the will of rulers and its violation considered as an attack on the body of the sovereign, which was answered in kind. Condemned criminals were publicly tortured before their executions. Although Michel Foucault (1977) is not concerned with the vicissitudes of compassion, his *Discipline and Punish* opens with a vivid description of public torture:

> On 2 March 1757 Damiens the regicide was condemned to make the *amende honorable* before the main door of the Church of Paris, where he was to be taken and conveyed in a cart, wearing nothing but a shirt, holding a torch of burning wax weighing two pounds; then, in the said cart, to the place de Greve, where, on the scaffold that will be erected there, the flesh will be torn from his breasts, arms, thighs and calves with red-hot pincers, his right hand, holding the knife with which he committed the said parricide, burnt with sulphur, and on those places where the flesh will be torn away, poured molten lead, boiling oil, burning resin, wax and sulphur melted together and then his body drawn and quartered by four horses and his limbs and body consumed by fire, reduced to ashes and his ashes thrown to the winds. Finally he was quartered. (3)

This display of public cruelty was the target of eighteenth-century reformers of criminal procedures like Cesare Beccaria (1986). In 1764, Beccaria wrote, "that the torture of the accused while his trial is still in progress is a cruel practice sanctioned by the usage of most nations" (29). Eighteenth-century reformers identified torture with a wholly rejected worldview, their arguments being made on moral as well as legal grounds (Peters 1985; Ruthven 1978). Partly as a result of writers like Beccaria, provisions for torture in the criminal codes of Europe were repealed, until by 1800 they hardly existed anywhere.

In the judicial system of the Middle Ages, pity took the form of mercy, which coexisted, without contradiction, with practices that humanitarians later regarded as "cruel." Criminals were not pardoned for causes. In Huizinga's words, "mercy has to be gratuitous, like the mercy of God" (1924, 25; see also Dülmen 1985, chapter 2).

With changed sensibilities, the experience of pain became more acute. None realized this change in the phenomenology of pain better than Nietzsche, who relates to the old willingness to endure pain as "a genuine seduction to life" (1968, 67). Nietzsche recognized clearly that it is not suffering as such that arouses indignation in modern culture, but its meaninglessness. Since there is neither a rational nor a sentimental justification for meaningless suffering or the unjustified inflicting of suffering on another, cruelty and the experience of pain became prototypical objects of the fight against it, whether in medicine or in the reform of the criminal justice system. (For medicine, see Pernick 1985; for the criminal justice system, see Ignatieff 1978 and Spierenberg 1984.) The capacity to identify with others, and in particular with others' pain, is promoted by the profound belief that others are similar to us. This identification is based on civic equality. Everyone shared the "hypersensitivity" of the middle classes. In democracy, everybody is formally in the same moral arena, which can be attributed to the condition of political equality, which made this moral state possible.

PAIN AND SOCIAL THEORY

In relation to pain, in social theory the place to start is with Nietzsche (1968) and Foucault (1977). Like Nietzsche before him, Foucault expresses skepticism about the value of eliminating pain (J. Miller 1990). Both believe that the modern state's attempt to eliminate pain in part prevents all struggle and therefore means the end of all human independence. Both also claim that the disappearance of externalized cruelty will lead to internalized forms of cruelty disguised in humanitarian rhetoric. Whereas for Enlightenment thinkers the elimination of pain (especially in the public arena) was the purpose of humanitarian reforms, Nietzsche and Foucault consider exactly this kind of elimination as inhuman:

> I regard the bad conscience as the serious illness that man was bound to contract under the stress of the most fundamental change he ever experienced—that change which occurred when he found himself finally enclosed within the walls of society and peace. (Nietzsche 1968, 84)

Thus does Nietzsche lament the dawn of the "humanitarian" age.

For Foucault, the history of reform over the last centuries is the desire of those in power to control and discipline society. He gives little credit to Enlightenment humanitarianism. In humanitarian reforms he sees an attempt to put people into sophisticated prisons of disciplining technologies. Modern human sciences have taken over the role of Christianity in disciplining the body. In this light, a shift occurs in the preferred subject of research not on reform to the reaction of pain but on the "reformers" and their disguised interests, those of control by a governing or ruling class. The ideals of the reformers are treated as ideology, in which the reformers imagine that their thinking is governed by logic and intellectual influences, while in reality manifesting class interest. This approach purposefully discounts the reformers' claims and their part in the "revolution of public sentiments." The "untamed other" is treated as representing the lower classes alone, to be disciplined so that capitalism may function more smoothly and efficiently. Shaftesbury described the unnatural passions

> as unnatural and inhuman delight in beholding torments, and in viewing distress, calamity, blood, massacre and destruction, with a peculiar joy and pleasure. . . . To delight in the *torture and pain* of other creatures indifferently, natives or foreigners, or of our own or of another species, kindred or no kindred, known or unknown, to feed as it were on death, and be entertained with dying agonies; this has nothing in it accountable in the way of self-interest or private good . . . but is wholly and

absolutely unnatural, as it is horrid and miserable. (quoted in Fiering 1976, 208, my emphasis)

Eighteenth-century philosophers of the Enlightenment further developed the ethics of "natural" compassion for fellow men. I have dealt earlier with Adam Smith, but it is time now to look at Jean-Jacques Rousseau as one of the main representative[s] of the idea of compassion as the basis for ethical conduct:

It is man's weakness which makes him sociable; it is our common miseries which turn our hearts to humanity. . . . [I]t follows from this that we are attached to our fellows less by the sentiment of their pleasures than by the sentiment of their pains, for we see far better in the latter the identity of our natures with theirs. . . . [I]f our common needs unite us by interest, our common miseries unite us by affection. . . . [I]magination puts us in the place of the miserable man rather than in that of the happy man. . . . [P]ity is sweet because, in putting ourselves in the place of the one who suffers, we nevertheless feel the pleasure of not suffering as he does. (Rousseau 1979, 221)

In Rousseau, the experience of common suffering became the new basis of humanity (Orwin 1996). Tocqueville contrasts with this democratic morality the social and historical limits of compassion, characteristic of the ancien régime. He quotes a letter by Madame de Sévigné that views with indifference, even humor, the suffering of peasants:

Do you want to hear the news from Rennes? A tax of one hundred thousand crowns has been imposed on the citizens, and if that sum is not found within twenty-four hours, it will be doubled and collected by the soldiers. They have chased everyone out and banished them from a whole main street, and forbidden anyone to receive them on pain of death; so one saw all these wretched people, women near their time, old men, and children, wandering in tears out of town, not knowing where to go, without food, without bedding. The day before yesterday they broke on the wheel the fiddler who started the dance and the stealing of stamped paper; he was quartered . . . and his limbs exposed at the four corners of the town. . . . They have taken sixty townsmen and will start hanging them tomorrow. . . . You talk very cheerily about our miseries; we are not so broken on the wheel now; once in a week, to keep justice going; it is true that hanging now seems quite a treat. (Tocqueville 1969, 563)

The imagination of suffering is therefore part of the democratic project. Pain and the struggle against it became so central in Enlightenment and liberal thought that one observer claimed, "Liberalism, perhaps to a greater degree than any other political theory, first revealed how exposed were the nerve ends of modern man, how heightened his sensitivity to pain" (Wolin 1960, 326).

On this ground, Bentham (1969) developed a moral theory at the end of the eighteenth century that identified evil with pain. If all pain is considered evil, then not even the pain of animals can be excluded from the scope of compassion. Therefore, underlying the emergence of "natural" and public compassion was a change in the understanding of pain and pleasure (Pernick 1985).

ANIMAL AND CHILD PROTECTION
AS EDUCATION OF SENTIMENTS

I will look now at how these sentiments emerged historically toward very special groups, namely animals and children.

Since there is neither a rational nor a sentimental justification for meaningless suffering or the unjustified inflicting of suffering on another—"cruelty"— innocent animals and children became prototypical objects of compassion. Lacking agency, both are ideal victims. This is also what distinguishes animals and children from other objects of compassion, such as prisoners and the adult poor; here, compassion is mixed with moral indignation, whereas animals and children are solely victims. The reform of treatment of animals is significant for policy toward humans. If animals are outside human concern then this viewpoint also legitimized the ill-treatment of those who were in an animal-like condition. The main point is the animal's capacity to suffer. Animal metaphors, previously signaling disgust and moral revulsion, were changed to signal compassion and a definition of human victims lacking agency and therefore not to be reproached for misconduct.

Thus, old arguments against cruelty to animals were man-centered. However, a more radical view developed: cruelty to animals was wrong in itself, causing pain to animals, without taking into account any consequences for humans. One of the intellectual turning points in this shift was the publication in 1776 in London of *A Dissertation on the Duty of Mercy and Sin of Cruelty to Brute Animals*, by the Reverend Humphrey Primatt:

> Superiority of rank or station exempts no creature from the sensibility of pain, nor does inferiority render the feelings thereof the less exquisite. Pain is pain, whether it be inflicted on man or on beast; and the creature that suffers it, whether man or beast being sensible of the misery of it while it lasts, suffers Evil. (quoted in Turner 1980, 11)

What was new in Primatt's thinking, informing compassionate behavior toward animals, was the imputation of suffering and pain to animals. The feelings of suffering objects, rather than their intelligence or moral capacity, came to define a claim on others' compassion. Many other tracts were published in England and the United States emphasizing considerate treatment of animals. Some examples are: John Hildrop, *Free Thoughts upon the Brute Creation* (1742); Richard Dean, *Essay on the Future Life of Brute Creatures* (1768); and the Reverend James Granger's 1772 sermon, *An Apology for the Brute Creation* (for more information on these works, see Gharpure 1935). The tone of these writings was that animals had feelings, which called for moral respect. Both animals and children were marginalized in a rapidly growing process of industrialization, which rendered them increasingly useless in economic terms. Animal rights and children's rights were part of the same agenda. Both are passive objects of others' concern, unable to speak for themselves. Children and animals also shared a moral dependence and vulnerability that appealed to the nobility of compassionate persons or groups; this was not always the case. In medieval Europe and colonial America, as in biblical times, animals were invested with human rights and responsibilities. They were tried in court and even testified. Animals were executed for legal transgressions. (On animals as "legal persons" in premodern times, see Berkenhoff 1937; Carson 1972; Evans 1884; Ritvo 1987.) In the American colonies, these legal procedures against animals were most often used in cases of bestiality. One example is the hanging of a woman and a dog together for this very crime in 1679 in Tyburn (Thomas 1983, 98). By the nineteenth century, authorities in Europe and the United States stopped sentencing animals to die for their "crimes."

In rural society, farm as well as domestic animals and men lived in familiar closeness with each other. Language expressed this sense of closeness. Many descriptive terms applied equally to men and beasts. Children were "kids," "cubs," or "urchins" (a later very popular term with reformers, who referred to poor children as "street urchins"). Urban life, of course, eroded this familiarity. As children were sentimentalized in the families of the middle classes, so were animals. Pets were a normal feature of middle-class households, especially in towns, where animals had lost their useful functions. Animals were kept for emotional gratification, allowed into the house, and given a personal name.

However, a distinction must be drawn between the daily interaction of humans with their animals and theological thought addressing the question of cruelty to animals (Passmore 1975). Christian theology condemned cruel behavior to animals on the grounds that it brutalized human behavior. Any pleasure that it might give to humans was condemned; cruelty to animals in itself was not at issue. Christian theology rejected all forms of naturalism, implying an absolute barrier between humans and animals. This absolute distinction between men and animals was also a feature of the philosophy of Descartes. For him, animals were machinelike, devoid of feeling and soul. Thought and feeling, both attributes of the soul, were denied to animals. Without soul, animals were not able to suffer. Thus Hogarth's famous engravings, *The Four Stages of Cruelty* (1751), showed in very detailed form how cruelty to animals develops into cruelty to men. Animal suffering as such was not his concern. He wanted to illustrate the spiritual and moral corruption of his time (Levie 1947).

Animal lovers and pedagogues shared the attitude that the first sentiment of animals and children is that of pain and suffering. As in the case of the abolition of slavery and the slave trade, and the reforms of prisons and lunatic asylums, the English movement for the prevention of cruelty to animals was started by the Free Churches (Levie 1947, 48ff). Their clergy preached kindness to animals as they preached kindness as a moral virtue in general. Diffusing from there, the sentiment of compassion toward animals became a theme in English literature, as with compassion toward children (Schöffler 1922). The new child-literature of the eighteenth century used animals as a didactic means, to infuse benevolence. Children needed lessons in compassion and fellow feeling, and the proper treatment of animals became a recurrent didactic theme. Most of these books depicted bad and good boys, the bad boys torturing animals, the good ones coming to the animals' defense (Harwood 1928, 250–60).

This attitude was made possible by the reevaluation of original sin in relation to children and of animals' criminal responsibility. What distinguishes animals and children from others is their complete "innocence." On the other hand, all objects of public compassion had been attributed animal-like qualities. Immigrants and blacks were referred to in terms reminiscent of animals—they lived like "beasts." Infants were like animals without language; women were often closer to the condition of nature and thus to animals. The poor, especially, were often compared with beasts: ignorant, irreligious, squalid in their living conditions (Thomas 1983, 44ff). In the reform of animal treatment, compassion toward the suffering of humans was highly significant. Compassion for animals was an important move toward an impersonal and detached compassion for the sufferings of other humans.

Organized movements against cruelty to animals were founded in Europe and the United States during the course of the nineteenth century. The first was founded in England in 1824, followed by societies founded in France (1845), Austria (1846), and Germany (1841). The American Society for the Prevention of Cruelty to Animals (ASPCA) was founded by Henry Bergh in 1864 in New York City (McCrea 1910). Although the modern idea of the prevention of cruelty to animals spread over Europe, it was particularly successful in England and later in the United States.

The success of the English organization was expressed in the passing of bills in 1835 (An Act to Consolidate and Amend the Several Laws Relating to the Cruel and Improper Treatment of Animals) and 1849 (The Act for the More Effectual Prevention of Cruelty to Animals; Ritvo 1987). The society in England, composed mainly of the professional middle classes, openly expressed their impatience with warlike traditions of the upper classes, rejecting hunting as a leisure activity. However, their main effort was directed against the working classes. Here they expressed outrage at the brutal treatment of animals both in work and at leisure. English workingmen, like their American counterparts, used animals as part of their recreational activities. Cockfighting, rat killing, baiting of wild animals were popular amusements. In America until the nineteenth century, cockfights were staged in amusement halls, and bull-and-bear fights were advertised in local newspapers. Dogfights were popular as well in some regions of the Northeast. In cities like New York, the most visible of animals was the horse. As the cities grew, more horses were needed for the expanding public and private transportation systems. In a survey of the life of the streetcar horse, the *New York Times* reported

in 1882, more than a decade after the founding of the ASPCA, already expressing the spirit of the organization:

> His time of misery must be held to date from the time he enters that service, when
> his poor feet never know what is to be off those horrible cobblestones. By the end
> of three years the ruin of the legs of most of these car horses has been completed,
> and then they are sold off to a large class who understand extracting the maximum
> of work with the minimum of food. All over the City may be seen animals attached
> to junk carts and dilapidated expresses, which literally have not a leg to stand upon.
> Watch the poor things for a moment standing, and you will see them shift painfully
> from leg to leg, as to give an occasion rest. Many are lame of both a fore and a hind
> foot, and cannot move without great distress. . . . A long way up town, near the East
> River, there is a market for animals of this kind, and any humane person attending
> it must reflect that the existence of horses is one of the most inscrutable in the ar-
> rangement of Providence. Here are animals, presumably innocent of offense, con-
> demned to long years of the extremest misery without remedy or appeal. For can
> any misery be greater than, with a weak, sick old body and terrible tender feet, to
> be attached to a heavy load driven by a man with a heavy whip, day after day.
> (quoted in Carson 1972, 91–92)

The *Times* reporter concluded that the horse was truly "a martyr to the industrial
age."

I have quoted this passage at length to give a taste of the moral language of
compassion prevailing in anticruelty societies. Important also is the personalized
language: "horse" can very well be substituted for any other suffering being, such
as "child." Twenty-five thousand streetcar horses died annually, and their treatment took over priority for the American Animal Protection Societies. One can
hardly argue that the concern for streetcar horses can be explained by the desire
to civilize and control the leisure activities of the working classes, as with bull-
baiting and cockfights. The suffering horse in the street was simply an affront to
the heightened sensibilities of middle-class men and women, who were less interested in civilizing other classes than in civilizing the public sphere through
which they moved while riding streetcars.

Before Henry Bergh began his campaign for animal protection, there were
some protective laws on the statute books of certain states. The New York legislature made cruelty to horses, sheep, and cattle a misdemeanor. Massachusetts
enacted a similar law in 1835, followed by Connecticut and Wisconsin in 1838.
However, they were hardly enforced. The first effective piece of legislation, accompanied by a machinery of enforcement, was the New York law of April 19,
1866, passed nine days after the incorporation of the ASPCA. It prohibited the
overloading, overdriving, and unnecessary beating, killing, mutilating, or maim-
ing of animals, and the failure to provide necessary and proper food, drink, and
shelter (McCrea 1910). The officers of the ASPCA tried to make sure that laws
would not be broken. An episode of founder Henry Bergh's life elucidates this
effort. Observing a horse given a brutal beating in the street, Bergh reportedly

stepped up to the driver, and the following dialogue was later recorded: "'My friend, you can't do that any more.' 'Can't beat my own horse, the devil I can't.' 'You are not aware, probably, that you are breaking the law, but you are. I have the new statute in my pocket; and the horse is yours only to treat kindly'" (Carson 1972, 97). Again it would be easy to replace the word "horse" with the word "child," particularly in the driver's remark that he was entitled to beat "his own" animal.

The annual reports of the ASPCA had in their concluding sections a list of prosecutions and convictions, in which one can observe the zealous activities of the society: people were fined and even arrested for carrying calves in carts, or for beating or whipping horses. As we learn from its first annual report, of 1867, the society established drinking fountains on street corners for horses, published little brochures, and Bergh himself lectured especially to children, urging them to treat animals kindly.

Who was Henry Bergh, the founder of this movement? Not a lot of material exists about him, but from the little there is (Steele 1942; Coleman 1924; Carson 1972), we know that he was born in New York City in 1823. His father, of German ancestry, was a shipyard owner and shipbuilder. Henry Bergh entered Columbia College in 1830 and according to his biographers lived the life of a young man of fashion, befitting his social background. He spent several years in Europe, and among other duties was appointed secretary of the U.S. Legation at St. Petersburg. His interest in anticruelty work was apparently awakened when he made the acquaintance of the Earl of Harrowby, president of the Royal Society for the Prevention of Cruelty to Animals in London. Bergh was the founder, president, lecturer, writer, and administrator of the equivalent organization in the United States, the ASPCA. People in his time referred to the cause as "Bergh's war." The ASPCA was called the "Bergh Society," its agents "Bergh's men." Bergh himself was empowered by the attorney general of the state of New York and the district attorney for New York City to represent them in all cases involving the law for the protection of animals.

Besides taking up the case of horses working in transportation, Bergh's and the society's activities concentrated on sporting activities as well. Although dog fights, ratting, cockfighting, and other sports involving the killing of animals had been illegal in New York state since 1856, these activities were still held on a nightly basis in pits, the most famous of which was Sportsmen's Hall, at 273 Water Street. In this sports arena, which held almost four hundred people, animals were baited against each other. The special attraction of the house was Reddy the Blacksmith, who would bite a rat in two for a glass of beer. Repeated raids on these establishments, instigated by the ASPCA in New York City and around the United States, drove these activities underground.

By 1910, the American Humane Association reported that 659 animal-protection societies had been formed in the United States for the prevention of cruelty. Of these, 247 were humane societies for both children and animals; the remainder were for the protection of animals only. These societies had an active membership of around 120,000 people in 1909. The term "humane" was used to describe the organized activities against animals, as well as for the benefit of children. Federation and unification of their work was sought through the founding of the American Humane Association in 1874.

The overall purpose of these societies was to diminish the brutalities of everyday life in the public sphere. The cruelty was ordinarily perpetrated in the public street, with insolent disregard for both the feelings of onlookers and the prohibitions of the law. Clearly, much of the pressure to eliminate the cruel sports stemmed from a desire to discipline the new working class into higher standards of public order and more industrious habits. Love for the brute creation was frequently combined with distaste for the habits of the lower orders. Membership was composed of the "respectable" groups of society. The SPCA can thus be seen as yet another middle-class campaign to civilize the lower orders. Kindness to animals was certainly a middle-class endeavor. Just as nineteenth-century working classes, dependent on the labor of their children, were reluctant to adopt the middle-class view that the growing child should be protectively insulated, so most workers related to animals in a rather functional light, uninhibited by sentiment. Compassion and a reluctance to inflict pain, whether on men or beasts, were identified by the reformers as distinctively civilized emotions. But more was at stake here; one of the arguments of the supporters of the SPCA was: "we are bound to reciprocate duties: brutes give us their labor, and in return, we are bound to provide them food and tender treatment" (quoted in Turner 1980, 54). It is interesting to note that part of the anticruelty campaigns against animals was expressed in the language of an ideal industrial morality of fair exchange. However, unlike other oppressed groups, neither animals nor children could make claims for their rights. So it would be difficult to argue that animals had been given more rights, since they didn't make any claims. Men's compassion restricted their rights to treat animals as they chose (see also the classical treatment on animal rights by Salt 1894). Public compassion and organized struggle against cruelty, therefore, as moral sentiments and translated into social action, attempted to restrict men's conduct and deprive them of what had previously been seen as "natural rights."

Whereas eighteenth-century poetry and literature expressed aversion to cruelty to animals in the literary and poetic spirit of the "men of feeling," nineteenth-century sentiments were expressed in activism and zealous drives by citizens to make the public streets a place of kind and gentle emotions. Cruelty to animals became private cruelty turned public. Compassion toward animals became the link through which these private sentiments became a matter of public concern.

WIFE TORTURE

When cruelty campaigns against animals became more successful, reformers and especially the members of the anticruelty societies turned their attention to a new issue. Cruelty to children became a public issue, and the idea that domestic relations between parent and child were immune from public regulations was attacked. This development was not restricted to the United States alone, but became part of public and political life all over western Europe as well. At the same time that cruelty to children and animals was being delegitimated, debates around wife-beating took shape as well. (The historical literature on wife-beating includes Gordon 1988; Grinwold 1986; Griswold 1986; Nadelhaft 1987; Pleck 1987.) In the antebellum period, debates over wife-beating were framed around the issue of drunkenness. The temperance movement was one of the first campaigns depicting a public willing to hear about the cruelties of domestic violence. Most temperance reformers argued against "male brutishness" caused by alcohol consumption, which they perceived as violating domestic ideals of middle-class marriage based upon companionship and sentiment. According to this ideal, men lost their rights to physically punish their wives. This development was paralleled by legal changes in the notion of domestic cruelty. So in 1874, Justice John Scott of the Illinois Supreme Court described the damage a husband inflicted upon his wife by his false allegation of infidelity:

> Cruel treatment does not always consist of actual violence. There are words of false accusations that inflict deeper anguish than physical injuries to the person—more enduring and lacerating to the wounded spirit of a gentle woman, than actual violence to the person, though severe. (quoted in Griswold 1986, 721)

This statement demonstrates the evolution of the concept of "marital cruelty" in the United States during the nineteenth century. Prior to the 1840s, the law defined cruelty as either violent threats or threats of violence. But slowly, the concept of "mental torment" became appropriate as well, and less-restrained definitions began to emerge under the impact of the middle-class ideal of marriage. Harsh behavior became part of cruel conduct. As with animal and child protection, these ideas moved back and forth between England and the United States. One of the most important contemporary articles on the issue of wife-beating was published 1878 in England by Frances Power Cobbe, a well-known reformer, especially in animal-protection movements. It was named "Wife-Torture in England," symbolizing also the expanded use of the concept of torture. Cobbe herself is aware of the expanded notion of torture:

> I have called this paper Wife-torture because I wish to impress my readers with the fact that the familiar term "wife-beating" conveys about as remote a notion of the extremity of the cruelty indicated as when candid and ingenious vivisectors talk of "scratching a newt's tail" when they refer to burning alive, or dissecting out the nerves of living dogs, or torturing ninety cats in one series of experiments. (Cobbe 1878, 72)

Cobbe also analyzed the phenomenon of cruelty to women as a particularly lower-class phenomenon:

> How does it come to pass while the better sort of Englishmen are thus exception-
> ally humane and considerate to women, the men of the lower class of the same nation
> are proverbial for their unparalleled brutality, till wife-beating, wife-torture, and
> wife-murder have become the opprobrium of the land? (Cobbe 1878, 56)

Much of Cobbe's article analyzes the relations between husbands and wives
in the lower classes in terms of precapitalist notions without ever actually naming
them as such. Husband and wife relations are like master–slave relations, where
husbands treat their wives as "things" rather than as persons. Her analysis echoes
that of John Stuart Mill, who in 1869 published his essay "The Subjection of
Women." There he likened the subjection of women to men to master–slave
relationships that could be resolved in the expansion of "sympathy" to the marital
relationship:

> when they are attached to one another, and are not too much unlike to begin with;
> the constant partaking in the same things, assisted by their sympathy, draws out the
> latent capacities of each for being interested in the things which were at first inter-
> esting only to the other; and works a gradual assimilation of the tastes and charac-
> ters to one another, partly by the insensible modification of each, but more by a real
> enriching of the two natures, each acquiring the tastes and capacities of the other
> in addition to its own. This often happens between two friends of the same sex, who
> are much associated in their daily life. (Mill 1975, 538–39)

Here Mill elaborates on Adam Smith's concept of sympathy and applies it not
only to gentlemen of civil society, but also to husband and wife. Friendship of
this order could only exist between those equal in excellence and moral capacity, precisely the reason why philosophers like Aristotle and others have denied
the capacity for such friendship to women (Shanley 1981).

Cobbe's and Mill's ideas were well-known in the United States. Cobbe's article was reprinted immediately after its publication in England in Lucy Stone's
Boston magazine, *Woman's Journal*. In this journal Stone published a weekly
catalog titled "Crimes against Women," where incidents of brutality against
women were listed and indicted. She also tried in vain to pass legislation in the
Massachusetts legislature to protect battered wives from their husbands. After that
failure, Stone began to lobby for physical punishment of wife-beaters. Others
joined in, and in the 1880s there was fierce campaigning in several states to introduce the "whipping-post" for convicted wife-beaters. Laws were actually
passed in three states: Maryland in 1882, Delaware in 1901, and Oregon in 1905.
The campaign was supported by several eminent male lawyers such as Robert
Adams, Simon Baldwin, and Clark Bell (Nadelhaft 1987; Pleck 1987). They
combined a strong sentiment for harsh punishment for all criminal offenders,
using anti-immigrant prejudices as their source for support. It is interesting to
note that this campaign was led almost exclusively by men. However, unlike
measures against cruelties toward children, the campaigns against wife-beating

had little institutionalized expression. There were no "wife-protection societies" founded, with the one exception of Chicago's Protective Agency for Women and Children, which was founded in 1885 (see Pleck 1987, 95–98). This society became in its time the most significant public organization to aid battered wives, but did not succeed like the child- and animal-protection agencies in founding a national umbrella organization. It can be argued that many of these issues were addressed indirectly through other efforts like temperance, child welfare, and several of the "social purity" campaigns, which tried to curb prostitution and pornography (Gordon 1988, 253ff).

The male involvement in such campaigns poses the question whether these strong sentiments against brutality and cruelty reflected a new image of manhood or a sense of superiority displayed by Americans toward newly arrived immigrants. This strongly displayed sense of superiority is probably the reason why some of the historical literature on these societies presents interpretations that stress the class background of the reformers and the reformed. Since most of the reformers were part of the middle and upper classes and most of the clients part of the working classes, these interpretations centered around guaranteeing the stability of the class structure of capitalism and controlling the unruly elements among the working classes. Anxiety about the loss of social order was another point of interpretation (Platt 1977; Katz 1986).

Also, Gordon (1988) emphasizes in her study on the Massachusetts Society for the Prevention of Cruelty to Children that "nineteenth-century reformers were more affected by class, ethnic, and urban anxieties" (28). These critics emphasize the illiberal elements of "child-protection" work by emphasizing the controls that were exercised over the rights of privacy of the family. This approach is often contrasted with a later "compassionate" approach, in which abusers are frequently seen as victims themselves (Rosenberger and Newberger 1979). This contrast between compassion and control informs much of the analysis of the evolution of child protection. The control model often relates to an aggressive use of intervention and an emphasis on punishment, very much like the work of the New York Society for the Prevention of Cruelty to Children, whereas the compassionate approach is identified with more therapeutic and rehabilitating measures, an approach identified with later various psychological/social-work approaches. Conceptually, "compassion" and "control" are seen here as inconsistent.

Other interpretations focused on the impact of the ideology of "domesticity" on men (see Carnes 1990; Griswold 1986; Rosenberg 1980; Rotundo 1987). Manhood in this interpretation was redefined for men to mean to become affectionate, considerate, loving, and compassionate husbands and fathers. Men became "feminized" (see also Kelly 1979). What eighteenth-century philosophers like Rousseau considered the education of the sentiments in order to reform the body politic became in romanticized notions of the nineteenth century "sentimentalism," often identified with soft female virtues. This strict division between reason and sentiment, or compassion and duty, has also been reinvigorated by some feminist writers, who attempt to revive the "separate sphere" argument of the nineteenth century without taking into account the historical conditions of its emergence (see especially Gilligan 1982; Noddings 1984). These analyses draw on the experience of motherhood to formulate an ethic of care and compassion. The "ethics of care" is expressed as a genuine feminine experience, whereas the Kantian ethics of "duty" and "principle" is defined as the language of the father or men in general. They claim that women define themselves in terms of caring and compassion as a counterforce to the instrumental and universal powers of the market powerfully expressed in the Kantian duty ethics (Lauritzen 1989). This thesis was put forward forcefully by Ann Douglas in her *The Feminization of American Culture* (1977). There she argues the close affinity between middle-class women and Protestant ministers in the transformation of the secular and theological culture of nineteenth-century American culture. She furthermore argues that the "masculine" values of economic expansion, urbanization, and industrialization were strongly countered by sentimental "feminine" values emphasizing cooperation, sharing, and compassion. Ministers and women became allies in their attempts to create a more sentimental society. In this interpretation, Calvinism in America was defeated by an anti-intellectual sentimentalism pushed forward by theologians and women. She charges liberalism with "emasculating" American culture, robbing it of its intellectual rigor and replacing firm theology with feebleminded sentimentality. Even the figure of Christ became in the course of the nineteenth century more and more effeminate. Love and self-denial, traditionally seen as attributes of Christ, became the attributes of women as well. A more "Gentle Jesus" was depicted in pictures as well praised in hymnals (DeJong 1986).

Compassion toward animals, children, beaten wives, and other victims of cruelty are seen therefore in this perspective as a female value, sponsored by women's reform movements in alliance with reformed Protestantism, counteracting "male" capitalism, which is rendered by definition compassionless. Men participating in these reform attempts are seen as "feminized" men, trying to rationalize callous capitalism through "feminine" activities. However, this understanding can only be maintained if one maintains an impermeable division between the spheres of the "home" and the "market," or the spheres of tough-minded business thinking and tender-minded aesthetic culture (see also Reynolds 1980). This bifurcation into a male-dominated world of capitalism and a female-dominated world of domesticity and sensibility, although extremely influential in the interpretations of reform attempts for children, obscures the origins of these reforms and the emergence of public compassion more generally. This bifurcation also relegates compassion to a sphere of impracticality, to noble deeds that are in the final analysis apolitical. Institutional changes for the benefit of the "miserable" in this view have been forced upon capitalist society by forces hostile and counteractive toward capitalism. However, compassion for children, as well for the poor and other "miserable" human beings (as well as animals) can also be considered as part of the rational conduct of capitalism itself. As Schumpeter (1942) observed: "our inherited sense of duty, deprived of its traditional basis, becomes focused in utilitarian ideas about the betterment of mankind. . . . Feminism, an essentially capitalist phenomenon, illustrates the point still more clearly" (127).

Jacob Riis, reformer and author of two books on children, *How the Other Half Lives* (1890) and *The Children of the Poor* (1892), combined this realism and optimism that characterized the spirit of compassion in his day:

> New York's poverty, its slums, and its suffering are the result of unprecedented growth with the consequent disorder and crowding. If the structure shows signs of being top-heavy, evidences are not wanting—they are multiplying day by day—that patient toilers are at work among the underpinnings. The good news was that, through many charitable efforts, the poor and the well-to-do have been brought closer together, in an every-day companionship that cannot but be productive of the best results, to the one who gives no less than the one who receives. (1892, 3)

It was not so much "feminine" sentimentality, but also the reformers' rejection of social Darwinism, which equated the economic struggle among humans with the struggle for survival among animals, that informed their views (Hofstaedter 1945). The social Darwinists believed that the poor were not to be assisted but should be left to die. Christian and other reformers rejected this view on moral grounds, based not on sentimentality alone, but on a view that saw the sufferer as a fellow human being. Reformers perceived themselves as unsentimental realists who rejected social Darwinism on the one hand and what they saw as soft sentimentalism toward the poor and deprived on the other hand. The rather unsentimental view is also clearly expressed in the words of Josephine Shaw Lowell, the founder of the New York Charity Organization Society:

> Human nature is so constituted that no working man can receive as a gift what he should learn by his own labor without a moral deterioration. No human being . . . will work to provide the means of living for himself if he can get a living in any other manner agreeable to himself. (quoted in Trattner 1989, 86)

Although compassion can be seen as a timeless and universal sentiment, its modern form in the shape of humanitarianism is to be understood in its connection to solving the "social question." Again, it was Tocqueville who noted this connection; in his chapter "Influence of Democracy on the Family" he noted:

> In countries organized on the basis of an aristocratic hierarchy, authority never addresses the whole of the governed directly. Men are linked one to the other and confine themselves to controlling those next on the chain. The rest follow. This applies to the family as well as to all associations with a leader. Aristocratic societies are, in truth, only concerned with the leader. It only controls the sons through the fathers; it rules him and he rules them. Hence the father has not only his natural right. He is given a political right to command. . . . In democracies, where the

long arm of the government reaches each particular man among the crowd separately to bend him to obedience to the common laws, there is no need for such an
intermediary. In the eyes of the law the father is only a citizen older and richer than
his sons. . . . Democracy loosens social ties, but it tightens natural ones. At the same
time as it separates citizens, it brings kindred closer together. (Tocqueville 1969,
586, 589)

Despite their intrinsic dependence, children, although prepolitical, were admit-
ted into the arena of public concern as citizens, sharing a universal human nature underlying civic equality.

This view of moral obligations was shared by nineteenth-century Protestants
and early-twentieth-century social thought. Both defined the possibility of a moral
community in terms of interaction between people of equal capacity. Congruent
with eighteenth-century concepts of sympathy and compassion, seen as "natural," moral behavior in the nineteenth century could be learned though interaction and intervention. The ideal claim was that a moral society was a socially
constructed reality that emerges from the interactions of persons with each other.
By practicing compassion people make themselves "good citizens." This also
legitimized "moral reform," since believers and/or members of civil society are
perceived to be redeemable in the religious or social sense. This aspect of redemp-
tion can include all species as animals, formerly excluded members of civil society like slaves, and of course children who moved to the center of moral re-
demption within the family. The Societies for the Prevention of Cruelty to
Children were only one of the many examples that characterized organized efforts to prevent moral and social decay. Out of these efforts emerged the charity-
organization movement. These organizations spread in the 1870s and 1880s
(Boyer 1978; Trattner 1989; Katz 1986). Essential to these organizations was the
so-called friendly visitor, usually a middle- or upper-class volunteer who visited
a poor family in order to establish ties of trust and friendship. The goal was to
cross the boundaries of class, religion, and nationality in a concerted effort called
"scientific charity." Proponents of "scientific charity" also worked closely with
early social scientists. One of the results of this cooperation was the examina-
tion of pauperism conducted by Charles Hoyt in 1874 and 1875. His survey of
poorhouses resulted in the removing of children from New York almshouses.

Belief in the ability of social groups to regulate themselves in order to become
moral lies at the basis of the new form of compassion typical of civil society:
public compassion. This is why social-reform movements were also moral reform movements. As Vidich and Lyman in their study on the Protestant shaping
of American sociology conclude, "virtually all the American sociologists con-
verted issues of theodicy into problems of sociodicy" (1985, 281). This shift is
also a shift to activism and moral reform, a shift "from prayer to praxis."

These Protestant sources of early American thought must be understood in
order to grasp the debates within the social sciences regarding social and moral
reform movements based on public compassion. An early generation of Ameri-

can social thinkers identified this moral regulation within the framework of a benign "social control" doctrine, in which social stability and moral cohesion could be guaranteed in mass society.

A typical spokesman of this tradition is Edward Allsworth Ross. In his seminal study *Social Control* (1910), Ross distinguishes between two kinds of instruments for social order, the ethical and the political. The ethical is composed of public opinion, suggestion, ideals, social religion, art, and social valuation, whereas the political instruments are laws, belief, ceremony, and education. Ross certainly prefers the ethical instruments and believes that they are characterized by a uniform, just, and homogeneous society, whereas political instruments of control are typical of hierarchical and unjust societies. Public compassion in such a vision is part of the emergence of a moral community. It also legitimizes direct interference into the lives of people when public compassion and rationality require it as justified. "Social control" in this vision not only produces moral order, but reduces irrationality in human behavior (Janowitz 1975).

The development of philanthropic societies provided that link of "public compassion," which enabled this moral sphere to emerge. Also, an encounter took place between the merger of humanist Enlightenment coupled with Christian morality and the middle-class need for order and security. The objects of moral reform were being defined in largely environmental terms. The success of reform now depended not on individual religious conversion, but on social and economic elevation. This development can be seen with particular clarity in reformers' increasing emphasis upon work with children, in contrast to their original concern for children's salvation. Movements against slavery and against cruelty to animals as well as temperance movements all expressed a desire for conformity to middle-class sensitivities, which they understood as the lessening of social distance and the restraint of affects and passions. Children were no exception. Their treatment became a public concern as well. In this regard "cruelty to children" became a threat to the entire moral sphere. Within this moral sphere of public compassion, debates about the correct way of dealing with the suffering of children continued. Should children be institutionalized, or should the family, even if unable to provide nurture and care for the child, be the sole caretaker of its biological children? How much responsibility should be granted to government legislation? The Societies for the Prevention of Cruelty to Children in the 1870s and 1880s had no hesitation in separating parents from their children, a view that from the 1890s became more and more delegitimized. This can be learned through a careful reading of the debates in the Proceedings of the Annual Conventions of the County Superintendents of the Poor of the State of New York. One of the county superintendents, H. C. Taylor, expressed this sentiment the following way:

If ever the world is to be saved from the influence of pauperism, however, it must be through the care of children of this same pauper. Our sympathies go out to the children of the poor, and should prompt us to redouble energy in their behalf. Our thoughts should not be so much occupied for the pauper and his support, as for

active, energetic and aggressive work in behalf of his offspring. (County Superintendents of the Poor of the State of New York 1895, 30)

It is this conception that justified intrusions on parental or private authority,
just as democracy legitimizes other restraints in other private domains. This perspective demonstrates as well how social (horizontal) control can turn into political (vertical) control, where public compassion is mediated by governmental
and bureaucratic rules and regulations from above. It also highlights consequent
debates among child-rescue workers and officials between the advocates of those
who favored separation between parents and children and those who argued in
favor of a family-rehabilitation model, which attempted to keep the child at home.
In the final analysis, social perceptions of pain are constantly mediated by these
mechanisms of social control.

Chapter 3

Cruelty to Children

I have shown that compassion acts as a mechanism involving people in democratic settings in a sphere of common morality. Compassion involves an active regard for the other person's welfare; a view of the other person as a fellow human being; and a response, which can be expressed emotionally and/or materially. It also means to transfer sentiments of compassion in organized social activity that translate the above-mentioned emotional state into activism. This question is best addressed by examining specific instances. I will discuss one instance of this issue by looking at attempts to alleviate the suffering of children, especially in the United States.

Movements against "cruelty to children" appeared in Western societies during the nineteenth century and continue in movements against "child abuse" today, albeit in a more bureaucratized and professionalized form. Compassion toward children presents an opportunity to study the emergence of public compassion from a unique perspective, since the relationships between adults and children are by definition asymmetrical and not reciprocal in the short term. I will focus here on the expression of collective interest in the moral and physical well-being of children. How did a concern for the children of others come about even as individualism triumphed? Why do people care about the children of strangers? In particular I am interested in reactions to the suffering of children. These reactions offer a rich empirical source for the study of the conditions under which public compassion comes into being. The theoretical work of Norbert Elias (1939, 1996) might provide us with some conceptual tools to understand these processes. The attempt of reformers to relieve the suffering of children is seen as part of a larger "civilizing process." In this process, Elias tries to draw a connection between the increased self-control of affections and passions and a new personality type that does not stand for cruelty. Part of the civilizing process is the growing emotional and spatial distance between children and adults. It is this distance that can turn them into the objects of reform.

45

One problem that appears constantly in this study is the question of whether public compassion and social control are really incompatible, as most contemporary sociological approaches seem to suggest. One of my theoretical purposes here is to press beyond the dichotomy between "moral progress" on the one hand and the "discourse of suspicion" on the other. The study of the emergence of public compassion toward children provides an opportunity to analyze these issues. One of the most crucial questions of liberal society asks who is responsible for others if individuals in civil society are primarily concerned with their own well-being.

My first contention is that compassion for the children of strangers is rooted in the emergence of the middle-class family. This family structure introduced new ideals and claims to tranquil domesticity and home life, guaranteeing its children a life with a future. Public compassion is seemingly contradictory, if we maintain a strict impermeable division between the two spheres of "home" and "market." The following analysis of reform movements that tried to save children of strangers from the evils of the city will enlighten us about the permeability of these two spheres. As the city became largely industrialized, children became less and less important to the production process. Child-labor legislation slowly moved them out of industry and into the household. In the middle-class mind, the streets of the city suddenly became threatening to children (Zelizer 1985). Moreover, in the newly privatized model of the middle-class family, children carried the aspirations of their parents for future repayment. Therefore, the development of "public compassion" for children must be understood in a broader context. It came about with the idea of "childhood" and of pedagogics as a new scientific discipline (as separate from philosophy and theology), beginning in the late eighteenth century and borne by the middle classes.

MIDDLE-CLASS SENTIMENTS AND THE FAMILY

The relatively new, powerful middle classes were the carriers of this responsibility and universal morality. The related idea of childhood developed as an integral part of the concept of the family as an exclusive sphere of privacy and intimacy, increasingly seen as responsible for the raising of children and for their moral development. Growing public concern for those children (and adults) who did not have a (complete) family or who were dealt with inadequately in their own family was simply the reverse side of this historical and social process. The "street" becomes the ultimate locus of vice and moral degeneration, whereas the home, with the primacy of the family, is the place where moral regulation supposedly takes place and virtue reigns. The street became the counterpoint of the notion of the home in the early nineteenth century. By 1830, ministers, schoolteachers, physicians, and poets alike were trying to teach their fellow citizens about good homes (Wright 1980, 1981). Better homes were supposed to strengthen family ties. Home was transformed from a place of dwelling to an island of security, warmth, and intimacy. Being "safe at home" was the idealized purpose of domesticity. This domesticity emerged as an element of middle-class awareness (Blumin 1989). The representative home should not be a stately mansion for the wealthy, but an average house for the families of the "middling sort." But domesticity was not only expressed in morally correct homes; it reflected an emotional attitude, a search for interiority not only of architecture, but of soul (Lukacs 1970; Rybczynski 1986). It became a sentimental search for meaning and security. A poem by the domestic writer Lydia Sigourney expresses this sentiment:

> For she, with harmonizing will,
> Her pleasures in her duties found,
> And strove, with still advancing skill
> To make her home's secluded bound
> An Eden refuge, sweet and blest.
> When weary, he returned for rest.
>   (Sigourney 1854, 31)

Home is turned into the refuge from a world of threat and insecurity. It reflects the interior landscape of the middle class not bound by tradition and custom but searching for new meanings and anchors in their lives. The dwellings, transformed into "homes," were supposed to provide both these anchors and settings for the interior life. Home became the locus of sentimentality, whereas the realm of rationality remained outside, in the world of commerce and business affairs. Each sphere of life was dependent upon the existence of the other.

The sensibilities of the middle class were manifested in a trust of its own achievement, a trust in the superiority of moderation, and a cult of interior values. Marriage was perceived as a community of spirit and emotion. Domesticity and the emotionally intense common life were held as a source of happiness and contentment. These love and marriage ideals could be seen most clearly in new ideals of child-rearing. Eighteenth-century debates in Europe attacked the praxis of leaving the children to domestics, and parents were admonished to raise their children themselves. Parents were also warned against the use of cruel corporal punishment, and mothers were strongly advised to breastfeed their children. Middle-class pedagogical theories were reflected in middle-class social theory and criticism. On the Continent, the struggle of the middle classes against the aristocracy, which based its predominance on birth and tradition, led middle-class thinkers to the question of "man per se" or "human nature." Small children were seen as "blank slates," uneducated and not yet capable of moral judgment, but educable and capable of learning moral understanding. Early childhood became a space apart from the sociability of earlier family forms. Sheltered from the eye of the community, the family ideal became an asocial space (Aries 1962; Degler 1980; Rosenbaum 1982; Stone 1979).

Another aspect of this historical development was the separation between home and work. The rationalization of work made it possible to restrict labor to certain hours of the day. The time-discipline of work also resulted in very strictly defined temporal spheres of nonwork or leisure. Not only were work and home physically segregated, they could also be identified as separate emotional or psychological entities. Home turned into a place and time where work was not done and, even more important, a refuge from the workplace. This perception of home as a refuge compensated for the struggles of the workday. The interiority of "home life" derived its meaning from this recompense. The consequences of the separation between home and work and between domestic and professional life were normative demands for emotions. The "discovery" of childhood was the glue of this domestic existence. For women, domesticity became existence, motherhood and female identity the same (Baker 1984; Bloch 1978).

In traditional work and life settings, the life of children was indistinguishable from the life of adults. Families lived and worked together. Children were part of the labor force of families. The parallel discovery of domesticity and childhood was characterized by the perception of a special stage of childhood, resulting in the spatial segregation of adults and children (nurseries). This was accompanied by intense emotional relationships between children and parents, especially between mother and child. Therefore, the conscious education of children received a special place. Children of the middle classes did not encounter the productive world of labor; they were going to be groomed for it. Self-constraint and self-discipline became part of the educational project of these social groups. This can also be seen in the rise of published materials warning against childhood masturbation that appeared in the Western world around the same time (Neuman 1975). Children of these families were more exposed to the influence of their mothers. For the most part fathers were absent during the day. Mothers slowly gained exclusive time with their children. Lydia Huntley Sigourney's *Letters to Mothers* (1838) illustrates aspects of the newfound and newly glorified relationship between mother and child:

> How entire and perfect is this dominion over the unformed character of your infant. Write what you will upon the printless tablet with your want of love. Hitherto your influence over your dearest friend, your most submissive servant, has known bounds and obstructions. Now you have over a new-born immortal almost that degree of power which the mind exercises over the body. . . . The period of this influence must indeed pass away; but while it lasts, make good use of it. (quoted in Douglas 1977, 75)

In Europe, the family-and-marriage model was primarily used as a political weapon against the aristocracy and its lifestyle of glamour and artificiality. Interiority and sentiment were used to combat exteriority and artifice. In America, the family model was not directed against a ruling aristocracy. It represented a "republican ideal," which expressed itself in the idea of the "republican family" based on equality and sentiment. Jay Fliegelman has shown how revolutionary rhetoric could be found in the language of family struggles. He points out the association of the familial rhetoric of the Revolutionary War with the ongoing rejection of seventeenth-century patriarchalism. The transformation of the family from an "institution for the transmission of a name" to a moral and spiritual function was part of the new political self-understanding of the new republic (Fliegelman 1982). The label of the "republican family" suggests the American variant of a larger transformation of western European family life. Under the sway of republican culture and politics, the home and the polity were supposed to display striking similarities (Grossberg 1985). These included rejection of unaccountable authority, the equation of property rights with independence, commitment to self-government, and the desire to think of human relations in contractual terms based on voluntary consent and reciprocal duties.

Through the restructuring of the middle-class family, privacy was turned into a positive good: the only true realm of freedom and self-development. On this ground, the public sphere is identified with the world of work, the market, competition, and politics, whereas the private one is the world of home, domesticity, and compassion. I will now demonstrate how these principles were being translated into public politics during the nineteenth century.

THE CHILDREN'S AID SOCIETY

One of the earliest reform movements dealing exclusively with the plight of children was the Children's Aid Society, founded in 1853 by Charles Loring Brace (Brace 1872; Bellingham 1983; Bender 1975; Boyer 1978; Stansell 1982). The activities of Brace can show us how compassion and fear were intertwined on the one hand and how compassion was exercised selectively on the other. Brace's foremost concern was with the potential destructiveness of the "dangerous classes" and their children. However, his and the society's methods differed substantially from earlier ways of dealing with delinquent and other potentially dangerous children. Prior to Brace, the usual way of dealing with socially problematic children was the asylum (Rothman 1971). Juvenile reformatories and "houses of refuge" were founded for this purpose. Rothman describes these institutions and how they were based on strict discipline and moral reform. These activities against children contradicted newly formulated concepts of childhood. Brace wanted to break with this tradition of institutionalization. He sought ways of preserving the natural influences of the family and social life as vehicles for reform. If the "natural" family of the child could not provide the nurturing atmosphere of the home, other parents had to be found:

The Boys' Sunday meetings, the teachings of the Industrial School and the words of our Visitors in their ministrations, have given the basis to our influence, which we sought to perfect, by what we regard as the great and especial work of the Society—the entire changing of circumstances of the children, by sending them to *new homes* in the country. It is evident often that no human power can save one of these street children, if it is left in its own circumstances. An unhealthy neighborhood, a squalid or a dissolute home, evil companions and vile parents, unite to surround the little one with such an atmosphere of poverty and crime, that very few can escape the effects of it. . . . We have wished to make every kind or religious family, who desired the responsibility, an Asylum or a Reformatory Institution, for the vagrant child; and, in the most effectual way, by individual influence, by throwing about the wild, neglected little outcast of the streets, the love and gentleness of home, and by bringing him up to honest, healthy labor. (Children's Aid Society 1855, 5, my emphasis)

On this basis, Brace adopted the "placing-out" system, by which children of the poor were shipped out mostly to the West, where they were supposed to work and be nurtured by good Christian families. Brace also sought volunteers from the respectable classes who would visit the homes of the poor and provide, in his opinion, a link of sympathy between the classes. Brace wrote of voluntary teachers:

Their self-denying efforts have brought in rich awards to themselves as well as to the poor. . . . [T]hey [the industrial schools] form a connecting link more and more in our artificial society, necessary, between the lowest poor and the rich, between the fortunate and the unfortunate. (Children's Aid Society 1857, 14)

Brace's sentiments toward these children were clearly influenced by the view that sentiments and moral virtue can only flourish within the domesticated home. Brace describes the anti-ideal of home:

On one of the frostiest days of this cold December, I was passing a block of tenement houses on First Avenue, when a boy and girl of some ten and twelve skipped out of an open door. They stopped a moment to look at some men digging around a gas-pipe in the street, and I had a chance of watching them. Both had little dirty baskets, evidently for picking up coal; they wore a thin jacket and ragged trousers which did not at all keep out the cold. The girl had a flimsy shawl thrown over her head, and a very slight looking dress; neither had shoes. Their faces were pale, but bright and joyous. I went up to them, and was soon in conversation. They seemed very cheerful, and not to care in the least for the cold. They were going out to get fuel for their mother, whose room they pointed out to me. They did not go to school, "cause they hadn't no shoes nor clothes!" I went up [to] the mother's room, at the very top of the building. . . . The place was very cheerless and bare, no fire in the stove, and hardly any furniture. . . . And yet, though for her pure young children too much could hardly be done, in such a woman there is little confidence to be put. In nine cases of ten, it is probable, some cursed vice has thus reduced her, and that, if her children be not separated from her, she will drag them down, too. (Children's Aid Society 1856, 27)

This very typical statement of Brace's clearly demonstrates that compassion felt for the children was not extended toward their parents. This exclusive form of compassion made it possible for Brace to willingly break up families whenever he saw it as necessary for saving the children.

By the mid 1890s the Children's Aid Society had placed out as many as ninety thousand children to families in the West. Brace's system of "placing out" had much in common with the colonial apprentice system, in that labor was to be given in return for room, board, and education. On the other hand, Brace departed from earlier traditions of institutionalization in the "houses of refuge." He sought ways of preserving and using the natural and spontaneous influences of family and social life as vehicles of reform. Aside from placing children in foster families, the Children's Aid Society established dormitories, reading rooms, and "industrial schools": workrooms where cobbling and other skills were taught.

However, Brace and the Children's Aid Society were not only concerned with ways in which parents treated children or defined their interests. Children were primarily regarded as problems largely in the context of the "dangerous classes," the large mass of unruly poor on the bottom rung of urban society. Thus, public compassion toward such children was also generated because they were seen as a menace to the social order.

The Children's Aid Society is also a very good example of the selective compassion typical of liberal society. Its principal idea was to break up the family in order to "save" the children. Children were to be emancipated from their ties to the milieu that was responsible for their misery. Childhood was also turned into a politicized concept (Bellingham 1983). A middle-class child framed by the concept of "home" was contrasted with the working-class child framed by the concept of the "street." Unlike their parents, working-class children were considered redeemable from their misery. Here Brace contested a prevailing opinion in New York that openly espoused a belief that it was best for children of paupers to die. Compassion was directed toward these children alone. Brace wrote in the opening statement of the society's Seventh Annual Report in 1860:

There is something about childish poverty that touches almost every one. We cannot connect it directly with laziness, or want of foresight, or vice, and the little sufferer seems to represent to us, for the time, social evils of whose distant influence it is the innocent victim. . . . We remember our own children, in what an atmosphere of love they live; how long it is before they know that any one in the world is even indifferent to them; how many appliances of science and luxury around them, to shield health and to make them comfortable; how guarded they are from temptation and trouble. And then our thoughts go back to what must have been the childhood of the ragged little creature before us. We fancy the first heavy sense of friendlessness and desertion; the unspoken sorrows which no one but the Infinite Father has seen; the heartache and loneliness; the tears that have wet the thin little face; the longings, which the child could not understand itself, for something or some one better than what it meets with; the struggle for bread, and the gradual harden-

ing of the nature in this bitter and wearying life. We can imagine how soon the sim-
plicity of childhood passes away. (Children's Aid Society 1860, 3)

Compassion was extended to these children because of their presumed innocence. But even more so, it was forthcoming through the juxtaposition of dominant notions of domesticity and idealizations of "home" that these children were
lacking. Compassion in the Children's Aid Society was directed exclusively toward the children, and this compassion generated a vastly different response in
regard to the parents. The deserved compassion for the children stood in sharp
contrast to the unworthiness of the parents:

> The parents [are] squalid, idle, intemperate, and shiftless. There they live, breeding
> each day pestilence and disease—scattering abroad over the city seeds of fearful
> sickness—raising a brood of vagrants and harlots—retorting on Society its neglect
> by cursing the bodies and souls of thousands whom they never knew and who never
> was them. Yet it is cheering . . . that the children are so much superior to the par-
> ents. (Children's Aid Society 1855, 35)

This was the beginning of welfare politics in the United States, which became
centered around the "deserving" child. This might be seen as a challenge to
democracy's claim of universal entitlement, since it means singling out a particular group, meeting its special needs even against its will, and granting compassion on a selective basis. The outcome of this selective process is that the children of the poor receive compassion, but there is no regard for their parents' plight
or surroundings.

THE SOCIETIES FOR THE PREVENTION
OF CRUELTY TO CHILDREN

I will now turn my attention to a later reform movement. With the foundation
of the Society for the Prevention of Cruelty to Children, the focus of child protection changed. Children received protection for their own sake and not because
they were seen as threats to an ordered society. The story of eight-year-old Mary
Ellen Wilson in 1874, in New York, is taken as a conventional turning point. Mary
Ellen had been repeatedly beaten with a cowhide. Mrs. Etta Wheeler, a church
worker in the tenements, noticed the child's cruel treatment. After several unsuc-
cessful efforts to involve the police, she appealed to officers of the local Society
for the Prevention of Cruelty to Animals. Two officers of the society came to Mary
Ellen's apartment, and under a writ of *de homine replegando* (an old English writ
of law applicable in certain conditions to secure the release of a person
from unlawful detention) took possession of the little girl. In court Mary Ellen
testified:

Mamma has been in the habit of whipping and beating me almost every day. She used to whip me with a twisted whip, a raw hide. The whip always left a black and blue mark on my body. . . . She stuck me with the scissors and cut me. . . . I do not know for what I was whipped—mamma never said anything to me when she whipped me. . . . I have no recollection of having been kissed by anyone—have never been kissed by mamma. I have never been taken on my mamma's lap and caressed or petted. (quoted in Bremner 1970, 185ff)

The case of Mary Ellen led to the foundation of the New York Society for the Prevention of Cruelty to Children, soon followed by two hundred such societies throughout the United States. "Cruelty" was the evil that the founders of these societies sought to exorcise. In the words of Elbridge Gerry, a founder of the society: "Cruelty to children produces mental and physical disease, and the prevention of such cruelty is a matter, therefore, of grave public importance" (Gerry 1883, 68). Cruelty within the home was transformed from a private to a public evil. Public interference in the lives of children was not new in the 1870s—think only of child labor legislation—but its focus changed. Until that time, there was little public concern with how parents treated their children.

In the movements to save children, images of childhood played a crucial role in the creating of public compassion. The "delinquent" child was one example. Reformers usually responded to delinquency by invoking legal institutions (the juvenile justice system, the asylum, etc.). Another image was the "deprived" child, immersed in poverty, ignorance, and unhealthy conditions (Rothman 1971). Here the goal of reform was to compensate for what was missing. With the foundation of Societies for the Prevention of Cruelty to Children the objective changed: protection *from* children was transformed into the protection *of* children. Its main goal was "protection from cruelty," which was understood as damaging to public morality. Cruelty became a public concern, and the child an "innocent victim."

Cruelty to children became a public issue, and the hitherto prevailing ideal that domestic relations between parent and child were sacrosanct was attacked. This development was not restricted to the United States but became part of public and political life in all western Europe. In England, liberals challenged the absolute power of parents over their children. John Stuart Mill wrote:

It is in the case of children, that misapplied notions of liberty are a real obstacle to the fulfillment by the State of its duties. . . . It still remains unrecognized, that to bring a child into existence without a fair prospect of being able, not only to provide food for its body, but instruction and training for its mind, is a moral crime, both against the unfortunate offspring and against society; and that if the parent does not fulfil this obligation, the State ought to see it fulfilled, at the charge, as far as possible, of the parent. (Mill 1976, 128)

Many local Societies for the Prevention of Cruelty to Children were founded in England in the early 1880s and eventually consolidated in 1899 into the

National Society for the Prevention of Cruelty to Children (Behlmer 1982). In France, Theophile Roussel headed a child-protection society, which succeeded, in 1889, to enact the Loi Roussel (*"Sur la protection des enfants maltraités ou moralment abandonnés"*), the same year the British Parliament passed the Act for the Prevention of Cruelty to Children. In France, the first societies for the protection of children were founded in Paris in 1865 and subsequently in Lyons. Back in England, from the 1840s until the end of the nineteenth century, intensive legislation was enacted that intended to protect children. Laws were passed in regard to child labor (1840–1841), unsanitary housing (1850), supervision of wet-nurses (1874), and compulsory education (1881). Beginning in 1857, there was a proliferation of societies for the protection of children: the Society for the Saving of the Children, founded in 1867 by Pauline Kergomard, aimed at reporting to the appropriate authorities and taking into public custody all children who were being ill-treated or in moral danger. Laws of 1889, 1898, and 1912 organized a gradual transfer of sovereignty from the "morally deficient" family to the body of philanthropic notables, magistrates, and children's doctors. The law of 1889 decreed that "fathers and mothers who, through their habitual drunkenness, their notorious and scandalous misconduct, compromise the safety, health, or morality of their children" would be deprived of their authority. It enabled police, social service, and medical authorities to decide which children should be taken from parents and made wards of the state. Between 1830 and 1860 the number of prosecutions for crimes and misdemeanors against children more than tripled. Reformers and public officials saw children as actual or potential victims of an adult society and in need of state protection (Donzelot 1979; Fuchs 1984; Meyer 1983; Weissbach 1989).

In Germany during the first half of the nineteenth century, initiatives for child and youth welfare started with the so-called *Rettungsbewegung* (rescue movement). In 1833 the first institution exclusively designed for children was founded in Hamburg under Johann Heinrich Wichern and called Das Rauhe Haus. Die Innere Mission (The Inner Mission) was added in 1848. The Rauhe Haus was the model that served Charles Loring Brace from the Children's Aid Society for his own work. The concept of the Rauhe Haus was to diagnose the danger of neglected children in industrializing cities (similar to the American concept of "dangerous classes"). Material misery, loss of familial authority, moral decay, and loss of religious faith all formed a single moral syndrome. Pedagogy in the Rauhe Haus was to compensate for all these deprivations. Wichern saw his work as closing the gap between the task of the state and the "love-task" of the church. Children had to be resocialized without brutality and violence. After 1848 Wichern wanted to coordinate his efforts, and founded the Centralausschuss für die Innere Mission. However, the number of private initiatives was hardly comparable to those in the United States and England. One example was the Kindesschutzkommission Sozialdemokratischer Frauen, founded in 1905 as part of the organization of Social Democratic women fighting child labor and later renamed the

Berliner Kinderschutzbund. At the end of the nineteenth century, several welfare laws concerning children were passed in Germany. Das Buergerliche Gesetzbuch (Civil Laws): Par 1666 BgB regulated parental authority for the first time throughout the country. Physical abuse of children was deemed a criminal act, and state intervention in cases of cruelty or neglect was authorized (Kuczynski 1968; Olk 1981; Peukert 1986; Scherpner 1966; Schwab 1971; Zenz 1979).

These brief illustrations from other countries clearly demonstrate that we are not talking about an isolated phenomenon but about a larger project of "civilization" and/or "discipline." I will now describe one particular project, the New York Society for the Prevention of Cruelty to Children.

THE NEW YORK SOCIETY FOR THE PREVENTION OF CRUELTY TO CHILDREN

After the Mary Ellen case, which precipitated taking action, Elbridge Gerry, a lawyer and legal advisor to the American Society for the Prevention of Cruelty to Animals, founded the New York Society for the Prevention of Cruelty to Children. The society's first annual report stated that although there existed a number of agencies serving children, none sought out and rescued neglected or cruelly treated children. The society's doctrine was summarized by Gerry:

> No matter how exalted the offender, the Society has the right to confront him with its proofs; no matter how degraded the object of its mercy, the society is bound by corporate duty to stretch out its hand and rescue from starvation, misery, cruelty and perhaps death, the helpless little child who ought to have a protector, but for some reason, not its fault, has been deprived of that advantage. . . . It is only when the parent exceeds the proper exercise of the parental functions, or omits or refuses to perform these functions, that the society protects the child against the parent. (quoted in Bremner 1970, 196)

Soon afterwards, the NYSPCC acquired police power and employed agents of the society in the city to look after children. In 1876, the society was instrumental in securing passage of an act to prevent employment of children. The society tried as well to combat child labor in most public arenas. At the society's request, the New York legislature passed the "anticruelty" act in 1881 (Laws of New York State 1881). Among other provisions, the act stated, "a person who, having the care or custody of a minor, causes or permits the minor's life to be endangered, or its health to be injured, or its morals to become depraved . . . is guilty of a misdemeanor" (see also Zelizer 1985, 195). The agents of the NYSPCC were given the power to enforce this act. The society also enforced the "baby-farming" law, passed in 1883. "Baby-farming" was the business of boarding unwanted infants in private homes until they died or were adopted or otherwise disposed of. Again the society was given police power to enforce the law:

It shall be lawful for the officers of any incorporated society for the prevention of cruelty to children at all reasonable times to enter and inspect the premises wherein such infants are so boarded, received or kept, and it is hereby made their duty to see that the provisions of this law are duly enforced. (quoted in Bremner 1970, 196)

The following summaries of cases the society dealt with are taken from its 1876 annual report. Hence we can follow how the officers of the society perceived their work, how they defined cruelty, and how they used the power of the law that the society helped create:

May 28, 1876: W.N. arrested for beating his son over the head with butt and heavy whip. Tried at Special Sessions June 1st, found guilty, sentenced to thirty days imprisonment.

June 26, 1876: Complaint of Mr. H. against H.G. for cruelly throwing a boy in basin of fountain in Washington Square, wetting child all over, then sending him home in that condition.

June 30, 1876: Complaint against A.S. and wife for cruelly beating and abusing their daughter. On investigation found that parents had only endeavored to control child and keep her home, she having gone home to live with persons not considered respectable.

July 29, 1876: K.M. made a complaint against her mother and sisters for beating and abusing her, her body showing marks of ill-treatment. An investigation proved the truth of the statement.

August 14, 1876: Complaint against J.M. for cruelly beating a boy named J.D. over the head with a club. Procured a warrant for arrest of offender Morgan, but upon going to arrest him, and secure attendance of the complainant, who was the aunt, and had charge of the boy, refused to appear and testify. The evidence being insufficient, the case was reluctantly abandoned.

September 18, 1876: L.B., Italian organ grinder, arrested for having in charge for begging, a child eleven years old, named G.B. Tried September 21st Special Sessions; guilty, sentenced fifty dollars fine.

Such examples were repeated in the succeeding annual reports. In its first ten years, the society handled sixteen thousand cases involving more than fifty thousand children. After ten years of activity, Elbridge Gerry gave a presidential address:

Ten years ago in this city an atrocious case of cruelty to a child called this Society into existence. The children of the poor then had no protector. Impecunious parents drove them from their miserable homes at all hours of the day and night to beg and steal.

They were trained as acrobats at the risk of life and limb, and beaten cruelly if they failed. They were sent at night to procure liquor for parents too drunk to venture themselves into the streets. . . . Their surroundings were those of vice, profanity and obscenity. Their only amusements were the dance halls, the cheap theaters and museums and the salons. Their acquaintances were those hardened in sin. . . . The question of their health, of their education, of their morals and religious culture was entirely lost sight of. . . . The general supposition, or rather presumption, was, that every parent knew and did what was best for the welfare of the child, and that no outside person had any right whatever to interfere. Hence, the reluctance of public officials to meddle in what was deemed the most sacred of existing relations, in very many cases rendered the child helpless against those who, under cover of parental authority, abused its legal rights. (New York Society for the Prevention of Cruelty to Children 1885)

Public compassion is here mediated by governmental and bureaucratic rules and regulations from above. This statement indicates clearly that public policy regulating the lives of families and aimed at the protection of children within the family is not only interference in the private lives of families, but extends to excluded members of civil society.

PROPER TREATMENT OF CHILDREN AS MORAL SENTIMENT

With civil society, the nature of compassion changed. This suggests a transformation of moral sentiments, a revolution in sensitivity, a civilizing process in Elias's terms. Previously accepted conduct was deemed unacceptable. At the same time, standards of middle-class parental discipline of children were imposed on other classes. The proper treatment of children became part of a "civilized" moral attitude, legitimizing "reform" in order to "civilize" and "discipline." Thus, the enforced attempt at changing parents' conduct toward children was the result of a "civilizing process" for the reformers, but should be better termed a "civilizing offensive" toward the reformed (Krieken 1990). Changing concepts about children and changing perceptions of the role of the family helped to create the legal entity of the cruelly treated child. By 1890, the New York Society for the Prevention of Cruelty to Children became the principal agency controlling the reception, care, and disposition of neglected and abused children in that city (Folks 1902). It had in its care an average of approximately fifteen thousand children. However, one of the earliest critics of the society, Homer Folks, remarked as early as 1902:

Without detracting from the great credit due to such societies for the rescue of children from cruel parents or immoral surroundings, it must be said that their influence in the upbuilding of very large institutions, and their very general failure to urge the benefits of adoption for young children, have been unfortunate. Probably their greatest beneficence has been, not to the children who have come under their care, but to the vastly larger number whose parents have restrained angry tempers and vicious impulses through fear of "the Cruelty." (Folks 1902, 175)

Although differing over what should be done for children, Folks acknowledged that the society "civilized" many parents. Compassion for children was therefore closely connected with indignation toward the parents. This was also mixed with a strong sense of superiority toward the mostly working-class and immigrant parents that composed the clientele of the society. Thus, in the Eleventh Annual Report Gerry stated that most "cruelists were not Americans," and that the ill treatment of children was perpetrated mostly by people who were foreign to the "civilized American way" (New York Society for the Prevention of Cruelty to Children 1886, 6–7). Gerry, in an article published in 1895, also proposed severe physical punishment for offenders against children and women (Gerry 1895). In this article, Gerry drew parallels between those who are cruel to children and those who are cruel to women. He referred to both types as "uncivilized."

THE MEANING OF COMPASSION IN NINETEENTH-CENTURY "CHILD SAVING"

What is the meaning of these campaigns? Are they expressions of humanitarianism, or can they be seen as manifestations of sentimentality, or even as cool and calculated attempts at increasing the power of one class over another? Can they be both? The strongly displayed sense of superiority of the reformers probably accounts for the fact that some of the historical literature on these societies presents interpretations that stress the class backgrounds of the reformers and the reformed. Since most of the reformers were in the middle and upper classes and most of the clients in the working classes, these interpretations center around guaranteeing the stability of the class structure of capitalism and controlling unruly elements. Anxieties about the loss of social order is another point of interpretation (Katz 1986; Platt 1977).

Michael Katz (1986) writes:

> The SPCC represented more than another intrusion into the lives of the very poor. It embodied a prevailing consensus that the most effective manner to root out pauperism was to break up families. At the same time, it fermented suspicion, hostility, and disunity among the poor of great cities by encouraging neighbors to spy on and accuse one another. (109)

Gordon (1988) also points out in her study on the Massachusetts Society for the Prevention of Cruelty to Children that "nineteenth-century reformers were more affected by class, ethnic, and urban anxieties" (28). These critics stressed the illiberal elements of "child protection" work by emphasizing the controls that were exercised over the rights of privacy of the family. This approach is often contrasted to a later "compassionate" approach, in which cruel parents are frequently seen as victims (Rosenberger and Newberger 1979). This contrast between compassion and control informs much of the analysis of the evolution of child protection. The control model often relates to an aggressive use of intervention and an emphasis on punishment very similar to the work of the New York

Society for the Prevention of Cruelty to Children. The compassionate approach, on the other hand, is identified with more therapeutic and rehabilitating measures and is an approach that comes closer to later social-work approaches. Conceptually, "compassion" and "control" are seen here as incompatible. This view is also shared by Foucault. Control was, for him, the guiding principle of reform. Foucault gives little credit to Enlightenment humanitarianism. In humanitarian reforms he sees an attempt to put people into sophisticated prisons of disciplining technologies. Modern human sciences have taken over the role of Christianity in disciplining the body. He furthermore claims that the disappearance of externalized cruelty will lead to internalized forms of cruelty disguised in humanitarian rhetoric. Whereas Enlightenment thinkers viewed the elimination of pain, especially in the public arena, as the purpose of humanitarian reforms, Foucault held that control excludes respect for the reformed and contains the desire to dominate peoples' bodies and souls. He depicts two systems of power: classical and modern (see Spierenburg 1984).

Not completely disagreeing with Foucault, Elias (1978) believes that restraints on impulses and more complete control of emotions parallel the increasing interdependence of men based on formal and legal equality typical of civil society. Here, increased sensitivity toward the suffering of others means the concomitant exercise of more control. In this more liberal vision of social control, humanitarianism is part of a larger middle-class project based on the ideals of public compassion and the desire to reduce irrationality and cruelty. This demands distance between members of civil society. As shown above, new concepts of childhood created this space between children and adults. The distance between people necessitates the eradication of violence from the public sphere. Furthermore, the increasing standards of self-control are to be expanded to others. This view attempts to counter the self-interested individualistic views of "economic man" trying to maximize utility at all costs. Studying the activities of the anti-cruelty societies also presents us with a paradox. It is impossible to speak about interference in the lives of families with clear-cut certainty. We must see the family as being divided between children and parents. Children often went to the offices of the society to complain about the cruel conduct of their parents. Children found a voice. It was not exactly their own voice, but the voice of class-conscious reformers interested in both maintaining social order and transforming the "consciences" of the reformed. Here we are presented with a vision of morality that emerges within market society, a vision that goes beyond the dichotomy of "good intentions" and the desire to control. The development of philanthropic societies provided the crucial link of "public compassion" that enabled this particular moral sphere to emerge. The proper treatment of children became a public concern. The public stage for child concern was set for years to come. So was the conceptual dichotomy between compassion and control.

Chapter 4

Democracy and Child Welfare

It is time now to look more closely at the connection between compassion and democracy. As we have seen, compassion is not simply an abstract feeling; it is practical humanitarianism. Many people have argued that moral sentiments like compassion are distinctively modern and have social origins. But this does not mean, at least in this study, that they are simply a ruse of the ruling class. Rather it means that moral sentiments emerged in a specific historical and social context: the rise and consolidation of capitalism (Haskell 1985). This sounds, at least on the first hearing, counterintuitive. But we should not forget that the market is more than just a way to organize economic relations. The market allows people to enter, independent of their will, into universal moral relationships. The market expands the horizons of people's moral responsibility, which were formerly limited by exclusivist bonds of memberships in corporate groups. Humanitarianism thus emerges from market relationships.

Ideally, in a market society everyone is a potential partner, and this potential universality expands our horizons of humanity from exclusive bonds to universal ones. Moral obligations are not solely internal restraints, nor are they simply self-conscious deceptions in order to attain some goal; they are, at least in part, the reflection of an expanded sphere of action. It is true that a major part of the reform of manners did involve the transition from hierarchical control to the internalization of mores (Thompson 1981). But it was for this very reason that the process of moral reform had to involve the reformation of the manners of all parts of society. It could not simply be the action of a dominant class on the classes below.

I suggest, therefore, that with the lessening of categorical and corporate social distinctions, compassion becomes more extensive. The capacity to identify with others is promoted by the profound belief that they are similar to us. This underlying emotional identification is based on the political structures of civic equality. And historically, the growth of identification has been reciprocally connected with the growth of civic equality.

This chapter will follow the way in which changes in the moral sentiment toward children were reflected in changes in child-welfare law. It will closely listen to the voices of the reformers themselves, in order to give voice to a perspective that has been neglected in recent studies on reform. And it will emphasize that the discourse of compassion was integrally bound up with a new discourse on democracy during a decisive moment in the history of the United States, but not only there.

FROM PRIVATE TO PUBLIC WELFARE

The turn of the century was the end of the "heroic" age of voluntarism. By this time, compassion was no longer thought of as an individual attribute, but a rather universal attribute—as an attribute of a good society rather than of a good man. This notion of compassion was mediated by the professionalization of charity work into social work. But around this time, the new concept of public welfare could still clash with the older tradition of voluntarism and private relief. These clashes shed light on the question of how and why these changes occurred.

I focus on three major contested issues regarding child welfare and cruelty to children: the mothers'-pensions movement; the emergence of the juvenile court; and the reform of child-labor legislation. These efforts illustrate the "progress" of compassion in the direction of passionless and rational policies. Each of these efforts to mitigate cruelty to children was contested. In fact, they led to major controversies over the distinction between public and private authority. These disputes were not only about the state's responsibility for proper child-raising, or the expansion of a "paternalistic" state into the private lives of families. Given the force of the public–private distinction in liberal ideology, and that of the newly privatized family on the middle-class model, it is not surprising that these disputes were deeply entangled in debates about the proper scope of citizenship and democracy. The course of these disputes illustrates the power of public concern and how it resulted in the institutionalized compassion of state policies.

A central issue in child-welfare efforts during the Progressive era was how children could be saved while the unity of the family was preserved. Though this seems like an obvious dilemma to modern readers, it was a sharp break from former policies. Previously, the breaking up of the natural family was regarded as a solution, as the obvious way to save suffering children from cruel parents. But now, one of the central questions became whether to fund families so as to allow poor children to remain with their parents. The new goal of child-welfare reform was to reduce the number of dependent children in institutions and foster homes. The old policy was that of the New York Society for the Prevention of Cruelty to Children (NYSPCC). The new agenda became official policy when the Massachusetts Society for the Prevention of Cruelty to Children (MSPCC), led by Carl Carstens, became the leading child-welfare organization. The transition from the NYSPCC to the MSPCC was the transition from punitive action to prevention.

DEMOCRACY AND CITIZENSHIP

Much of this debate is discussed in an influential essay by C. B. MacPherson titled "Democratic Theory: Ontology and Technology." MacPherson (1973) claims that the ontological assumptions of Western democratic theory are composed of two basic and contradictory assumptions: that humans are consumers, and that humans exercise uniquely human attributes. MacPherson thinks that capitalist society does not allow the second, ethical conception of human capacity to develop, and that there is therefore a necessary tension between the development of capitalism and the development of democracy.

It was exactly this problem that some social theorists at the turn of the twentieth century set out to solve. Child-welfare reformers tried to find a policy that reconciled the individual rights of the child with its unique dependence on its family. At a higher level of abstraction, social theorists formulated ideal claims that sought to safeguard the principles of individual liberty while integrating them into a community. In other words, they were trying to formulate an individualist theory of community, and what they came up with was moral citizenship. This notion combined two principles of liberty that MacPherson considers irreconcilable: positive and negative liberty (Berlin 1965). Negative liberty is "the area within which a man can act unobstructed by others," whereas positive liberty "derives from the wish on the part of the individual to be his own master."

Between 1870 and 1920, political and social thinkers in Europe and America created a discourse that combined these two principles in theory, and they inspired social reformers to formulate political agendas and policies based on a middle ground between laissez-faire capitalism and socialism (Kloppenberg 1986). Thomas Hill Green and Leonard Hobhouse in England, and John Dewey in America, are prominent in this school. Their ideas offer a context in which the ideals and practices of reformers, including welfare reformers, can be clearly understood.

Green made a seminal statement in his 1881 Lecture on Liberal Legislation and Freedom of Contract. Therein he defended the notion of "positive freedom" against the laissez-faire freedom of contract:

> When we speak of freedom as something to be so highly prized, we mean a positive power or capacity of doing or enjoying something worth doing or enjoying, and that, too, something that we do or enjoy in common with others. We mean by it a power which each man exercises through the help or security given him by his fellow men, and which he in turn helps to secure for them. When we measure the progress of a society by its growth in freedom, we measure it by the increasing

development and exercise on the whole of those powers of contributing to social good which we believe the members of society to be endowed; in short, by the greater power on the part of the citizens as a body to make the best and most of themselves. (Green 1986, 199)

Green uses this notion of freedom as "development" to defend legislation curbing the freedom to employ children in factories as well as other restrictive measures of freedom of contract:

> The principle was established once and for all that parents were not allowed to do as they willed with their children, if they willed either to set them to work or to let them run wild without elementary education. Freedom of contract in respect of all dealings with the labor of children was so far limited. (198)

Green meant that although it was not the state's business to promote moral goodness in its citizens, it was the business of the state to maintain the conditions under which citizens could pursue the common good. "Self-realization" can be properly pursued only when the conditions binding citizens to each other are fulfilled. This individualistic theory of community does not just create a space for individual altruism, but rather makes it universal. Socially guaranteed altruism becomes a necessity for a well-ordered society because it is the condition of properly developed individuals. Universal compassion is based on, and in turn upholds, the principle of common citizenship.

Green held that these conditions were best fulfilled within market society. The market involves individuals in more and more complex chains of interdependence. However—and this was key—the market would have to be moralized in order to keep this virtuous circle going. Citizens would have to work for the common good, and to allow the state to curb freedom of contract, if they didn't want to lose their individual freedoms in a spiral of degeneration. But working for the "common good" was not only necessary to attain certain social goals. It was a moralizing process in itself that, once started and sustained, would keep society in balance and would allow individuals to develop their full moral worth. The concept of the "common good" in the strict sense concerns objects that cannot be obtained by competition. While the market provides the best possible conditions for its pursuit, it does not flow from market relations by itself. Benevolence is the goal and result of democracy and proper policy.

Green's ideas influenced the founders of the Charity Organization Society in England, which attempted to systematize and secularize the practice of religious charity. The founder of this organization, Charles Stewart Loch, was a student of Green's, and he relied on Green's ideas for the practical policies of his organization. Green's ideas about moral character and self-development influenced poor-relief and welfare on both sides of the Atlantic. The goal of charity was to help the poor to elevate themselves morally, so that they could become through their own efforts responsible civic members of the democratic community.

Ideals about moral citizenship and the reconciliation of freedom and morality were dominant in the ideas of the "New Liberalism" of the next generation (Collini 1979). In his *Liberalism* (1964), Hobhouse claimed, like Green, that society must provide for individual moral development. He also tried to defend the notion of positive liberty and its intrinsic link to social and moral reform:

> This is why there is no intrinsic and inevitable conflict between liberty and compulsion, but at bottom a mutual need. The object of compulsion is to secure the most favourable external conditions of inward growth and happiness so far as these conditions depend on combined action and uniform observance. The sphere of liberty is the sphere of growth itself. There is no true opposition between liberty as such and control as such, for every liberty rests on a corresponding act of control. The true opposition is between the control that cramps the personal life and the spiritual order, and the control that is aimed at securing the external and material conditions of their free and unimpeded development. (78)

Here, "control" is completely compatible with freedom, and can only be understood in the context of "ethical democracy," which is another name for society's capacity for self-regulation (Janowitz 1975). The fuller name for this kind of control is "social control." The adjective is of the utmost importance. Although today the term "social control" is often used to denote the regulation of society by the state, when the term originated, it was opposed to state control or religious control. It was not the control of some people by others, but rather the control of all people by all other people, of society by society, through various sorts of emotional hydraulics. The term had wide currency in the works of turn-of-the-century American sociologists, clergymen, and political theorists, all of whom were using the term to counter the increasingly Darwinian conceptions of laissez-faire that had by then become current (Fine 1956).

"Social control" and "ethical democracy" were the main concepts behind the reform movements of both Britain and America. In America, these ideas were expressed by none better than John Dewey (1859–1952). In an early essay, "The Ethics of Democracy" (1888), Dewey severely criticized atomistic conceptions of society and, echoing Green, advanced an ethical conception of democratic life. Like Green, Dewey emphasized the capacity of human beings for self-realization, capacities that could only be developed in concert with others within a democratic community. Consequently, human beings free to develop themselves individually naturally developed in common, and developed an interactive and mutually regulating community. Dewey rejected the notion of democracy as solely a procedural form of government: "Democracy, in a word, is a social, that is to say, an ethical conception, and upon its ethical significance is based its significance as governmental. Democracy is a form of government only because it is a form of moral and spiritual association" (240).

The equivalence of "social" with "moral" is at the heart of this perspective. A more integrated society results in more social human beings, with more possibilities of development, and more connections among them. The moral development of individuals is the reverse side of their increasing socialization. But this is only possible in an egalitarian society: "There is an individualism in democracy which there is not in aristocracy; but it is an ethical, not a numerical individualism; it is an individualism of freedom, of responsibility, of initiative to and for the ethical ideal, not an individualism of lawlessness" (244).

Only in democracy do all citizens participate equally, and therefore only in democracy is it possible to gain the ethical merits of a community based on freely choosing individuals. Dewey ends his essay in an almost mystical plea:

> The idea of democracy, the ideas of liberty, equality, and fraternity, represent a society in which the distinction between the spiritual and the secular has ceased, and, as in Greek theory, as in the Christian theory of the Kingdom of God, the church and the state, the divine and the human organization of society are one. (248)

When the social is merged with the moral, God—as the hidden spring of action, as the final court of appeal, and as the hand that regulates the ways of man—is replaced by Society.

Two principles of this ethical democracy are significant for reformers inspired by these ideas: "character," and the unity of the family. The obstacle to liberty is seen in flawed character. Therefore the fostering of character is regarded as the primary aim of all politics. The ideal citizen is self-reliant in both the moral and material senses.

Another leitmotif is the family. Dewey treated family affections on the same level as neighborliness, as the place where society and the individual most closely met. He believed—and he shared this idea with many of his contemporaries—that the family and peer groups provided a fulcrum point for moral reform, because strong local attachments lead to strong characters, which lead to strong communities:

> This is why the family and neighborhood, with all their deficiencies, have always been the chief agencies of nurture, the means by which dispositions are stably formed and ideas acquired which laid hold on the roots of character. The Great Community, in the sense of free and full intercommunications, is conceivable. (Dewey 1927, 211)

This idea also animated Charles Cooley's concepts of "primary group" and "primary ideals" as keys to democracy (Cooley 1962).

These progressive ideals were formulated in opposition to extreme laissez-faire capitalism and the social policy that went with it, a position best represented in sociology by the American Spencerian William Graham Sumner (1840–1910). Sumner attacked all forms of charity and philanthropy. He saw competition as the great regulator of social life. In this, he echoed the political economists of his time, who regarded state interference as a violation of human nature and the laws of economic development. These ideas of laissez-faire capitalism were countered not only by social and political theorists, but perhaps even more significantly by Protestant leaders who denounced them from their pulpits. During the later part of the nineteenth and earlier part of the twentieth century, this "Social Gospel" became a strong movement (Hopkins 1940; Gorell 1988; Danbom 1987). The Protestant leaders involved maintained that the Christian mission was being undermined by laissez-faire capitalism. The economic law of supply and demand was contrasted with the Christian law of love and compassion. As one of their leaders, Washington Gladden, put it:

> Now that slavery is out of the way, the questions that concern our free laborers are coming forward; and no intelligent man needs to be admonished of their urgency. They are not only questions of economy, they are in a large sense moral questions; nay, they touch the very marrow of that religion of good-will of which Christ was the founder. It is plain that the pulpit must have something to say about them. (quoted in Hopkins, 24)

The congruence of the movement with the ideas of the new liberalism is well expressed in a book by clergyman Lyman Abbott, *Christianity and Social Problems* (1896). Here he claims that the object of Christianity is human welfare; its method character-building. Charles Sheldon's book *In His Step: What Would Jesus Do,* published in 1896, sold 33 million copies by 1933 (see Hopkins 1940, 140–42). This book asks its readers to imagine themselves as Jesus Christ and ask themselves constantly what they would do in his place. In many of his examples, Jesus turns into a charity worker, visiting the poor and sick. The social teachings of Jesus became the primary focus of several publications of this time. Child-labor issues in particular received the attention of Social Gospel writers, and many were involved in child-labor committees around the country. Social Gospel leaders also regularly attended the meetings of the National Conference for Charities and were often asked to give a sermon on service and love on these occasions. The Social Gospel movement was a political ally of sociologists and reformers, an alliance expressed by their joint participation in the *Encyclopedia of Social Reform,* published in 1897 by William Dwight Bliss. This book became the handbook of social problems (and the policies proposed to deal with them) at the end of the century.

This trend toward sociologizing Christianity is most developed in the writings of Walter Rauschenbusch. His two main books, *Christianity and the Social Crisis* (1907) and *Christianizing the Social Order* (1912), were the most prominent expressions of the Social Gospel and provided a strong impetus for social reform. There he formulated the religious foundations for social reform. He argued that social justice and economic democracy were minimum requirements upon which a Christian social order could be built. He denounced the philosophy of laissez-faire as selfish, inhumane, un-Christian, unethical, immoral, and barbaric.

In the end, Protestant leaders, sociologists, political theorists, and journalists, in Europe and the United States, all combined in their attempt to formulate a middle path between laissez-faire capitalism and socialism. They were inspired by similar ideals and theories, and they converged on a similar agenda: to moralize market society through policies that would allow poor citizens to develop their capacities without becoming dependent on the means of relief. It was to be moral reform and social reform in one go; all of that was compressed into the charged word "reform." They emphasized that human beings have needs that reach beyond material ones (which they tried to encompass under the heading of development). But they also emphasized that these ideal needs could only be satisfied once a material and educational minimum had been provided. And lastly, they emphasized that a modern, democratic society of equals will only knit together if people have the means to develop, both individually and in common. To ignore the needs of the poor will corrode society to the point of crisis—besides being in itself evil and un-Christian.

MOTHERS' PENSIONS

From this perspective, family decisions clearly have both a social and an individual side. The contest between public and private interests came to a head in the debate over mothers' pensions (Skocpol 1992). By the turn of the century, public aid for dependent children had been proposed as an alternative to public outdoor relief and private charity. Beginning with Illinois in 1911, forty states adopted some kind of cash provisions for children without employable fathers (Leff 1973). These statewide programs culminated in the Aid to Dependent Children program under the Social Security Act of 1935. But although considered a success, the mothers'-pension movement did not proceed uncontested. The transfer of relief from the private to the public sector was challenged both by philanthropic organizations and by relief workers (Lubove 1986). Most of the opposition came from various charities in New York City (Smith 1987).

In 1897, State Senator John Francis Ahearn tried to introduce a reform bill in the New York state legislature to provide funds for destitute parents in New York City so that they could keep their own children at home instead of having them sent to institutions. The act was called the Destitute Mothers' Bill. Due to the opposition of all prominent charity leaders, the bill was not signed into law. The problem had grown acute by the end of the century because of an 1875 law requiring that children between three and sixteen be removed from poorhouses and placed into specially designed institutions for children. As a consequence, the number of children in institutions in New York state grew from 14,773 in 1875 to 32,542 in 1896 (Folks 1902; Schneider and Deutsch 1941). Sentiment against the institutionalization of children began to grow as well. The *New York Times* carried several articles between 1894 and 1897 pointing out the cruelties to children in these institutions. In January 1896 the *New York Times* ran several articles on the Westchester Temporary Home for the Indigent Child and its cruel superintendent. Apparently, several boys ran away from the home because they were beaten cruelly with a cat-o'-nine-tails. The *Times* expressed the sentiment that in institutions, there is no restraint of the parental instinct. Relating to the publications of the *Times,* the board of the State Aid Charities, in its Annual Report of 1896, condemned the superintendent and made clear that the use of chains for punishment constituted cruelty and should not be the practice in any institution of the state. These articles and the board's reactions indicate strong sentiments against institutionalization of children.

Homer Folks was one of the national leaders of the child-welfare movement. He started his career in the 1890s as superintendent of the Children's Aid Society in Philadelphia and later became the secretary of the New York Charities Aid Association. He gave a speech at the annual meeting of the National Conference on Charities and Corrections attacking the institutionalization of children that became a touchstone for child-welfare workers across the country. With Folks's speech, child-welfare workers came to a consensus that home life is superior to the life of institutions. But they could not reach consensus on how to create conditions that would enable children to remain at home. The debate about this problem gave rise to a new definition of *compassion,* wherein the new ideals of public welfare clashed with older traditions of voluntarism and private relief.

The major opposition to mothers' pensions came from the Charity Organization Society (COS). Founded in Buffalo in 1877 on the English model, by the turn of the century it had given rise to 138 local organizations in the United States. With Victorian faith, these organizations sought to elevate the principles of charity to an exact science—a science of compassion, so to speak. They strongly believed that the problem of poverty would not be solved by material relief, but through moral education of the poor. In their view, the soul of charity was not alms, but the visits that accompanied them. They believed that compassion was what linked individuals and associations of people and formed the bond that "pulled" the poor out of poverty. It could be organized and dispensed by voluntary "friendly visitors," but it could not animate the impersonal and professional actions of the state.

If voluntarism was their practice, religion was their theory. The system of "friendly visiting" had a long history in the practice of Christian charity. But "giving" in the Victorian Protestant version of charity was conditioned on the desire of the receiver for moral improvement; without that, help was not "deserved" and would not have the proper elevating effect.

Two statements formed the guidelines for the American Charity Organization in its fight against state-run poor relief: Josephine Shaw Lowell's *Public Relief and Public Charity* (1884) and Gurteen Humphrey's *A Handbook of Charity Organization* (1882). Lowell outlines her opposition to public relief by claiming: "Public out-door relief undermines the character of those it pretends to relieve, and at the same time drags down to their level those who never would be sufferers at all." She continues:

Human nature is so constituted that no man can receive as a gift what he should learn by his own labor without a moral deterioration, and the presence in the community of certain people living on public relief has the tendency to tempt others to sink to their degraded level. . . . [C]harity, then, as I define it, must be voluntary, free, beneficent action performed toward those who are in more destitute circumstances and inferior in worldly position. (66)

Gurteen Humphrey specifies the principle of "friendly visiting" of the poor:

The sympathy common in our humanity must be the basis. Friendship must in every case start with sympathy. The fact that the moral support of true friendship will, in the majority of cases, make alms-giving unnecessary, is one of the fundamental reasons why the visitor is required to abstain from the giving of relief. (177)

These were the grounds on which mothers' pensions were opposed by an older generation of charity workers. They believed that only private charity could reproduce the brotherhood of man undivided by classes and ethnic segregation. For the members of the COS, any form of public relief would perpetuate dependency by deteriorating character. It was therefore an impediment to the development of a free and democratic citizenry. They also believed that mothers' pensions would encourage men to leave their wives and children, cynically calling it "the shiftless father bill."

Welfare workers also saw in mothers' pensions an opening for socialism, a system they vehemently rejected. Thus, Edward Devine, secretary of the Charity Organization Society in New York, attacked them in 1913 "as an insidious attack upon the family, inimical to the welfare of the children and injurious to the character of parents . . . as illustrating all that is most objectionable in state Socialism." However, Devine understood that the tide was turning against private charity, and he offered a passionate warning:

I have no more right than any other to represent philanthropy as it has been understood by our fathers, no mandate to defend its representatives; but I cannot forbear to warn my friends who would lightly discard voluntary charity utterly from human society, that they are building upon the sand; that when they put their reliance entirely upon a self-contained, coercive system in which all the relief funds are raised by taxation and all are distributed arbitrarily on a per capita plan without reference to individual circumstances, without reference to the cooperation of relatives, of trade unions, of churches, or neighbors, without reference to any charitable agencies or social sources, they are making a violent break with the historical evolution of human society, they are following a will-o'-the wisp. (quoted in Bremner 1971, 379)

However, the old view of private charity lost out in this struggle. Private charity organizations successfully defeated attempts to institute mothers' pensions at the end of the century, but the growing institutionalization that was the fruit of that success turned public opinion against them. Between 1911 and 1920, more than forty states adopted mothers'-pension laws. With this change, children became indirect objects of the state's protection, through the mediation of the family. The family became the object of state policy.

The major impetus for the mothers'-pension movement came in 1909 with the first White House Conference on the Care of Dependent Children. Under the auspices of Theodore Roosevelt, more than 220 child-welfare workers were invited, composing the entire elite of the nation's official child savers. This conference was the beginning of federal-government policy regarding children, recognizing the care of dependent children as a national problem. Roosevelt delivered the keynote address, which expressed the new consensus of child-welfare workers:

> Home life is the highest and finest product of civilization. It is the great molding force of mind and character. Children should not be deprived of it except for urgent and compelling reasons. Parents of good character suffering from temporary misfortune, and above all deserving mothers fairly well able to work but deprived of the support of the normal breadwinner, should be given such aid as may be necessary to enable them to maintain suitable homes for the rearing of their children. . . . Except in unusual circumstances, the home should not be broken up for reasons of poverty, but only for considerations of inefficiency or immorality. (U.S. Senate 1909, 9–10)

Although the participants still could not agree on questions of private or public provision of aid, all emphatically stressed the importance of preserving the family of origin. It was this point that defeated the opponents of mothers' pensions—but their moral reservations, their distinction between the "deserving" and "undeserving" poor, and their fear for the characters of the poor would all find their way into the policies they originally opposed.

The basic principles of mothers' pensions were outlined by organizations like the New York Commission on Relief for Widowed Mothers in 1914:

> The Commission believes it to be fundamentally true that: 1. The Mother is the best guardian of her children. 2. Poverty is too big a problem for private philanthropy. 3. No woman, save in exceptional circumstances, can be both the home-maker and the bread-winner of the family. 4. Preventive work to be successful must concern itself with the child and the home. 5. Normal family life is the foundation of the State, and its conservation an inherent duty of government. (quoted in Bremner 1970, 379)

However, as with private charity, financial aid was not conceived as an end in itself. Most state laws had strong requirements describing the eligibility of parents for aid. To start with, the majority was designed for widows, and 82 percent of the aid-receiving mothers were widows. Provisions were different from state to state, but most states considered unmarried mothers ineligible. "Character" was still an important condition of aid. One commentator on the Massachusetts law declared, "The public authorities can make adequate relief a powerful lever to lift and keep mothers to high standards of home care. If we grant aid to a woman whose care of her children will just pass muster, we throw away a chance to make these women improve" (quoted in Tiffin 1982). Mothers had to adjust their conduct. Children were regarded as the future citizens of the state and their socialization a public matter. Although administered by the state, the moral demands that were characteristic of the old Charity Organization Society were continued.

As a consequence of the 1909 White House Conference, an act of Congress established the U.S. Children's Bureau in 1912. It had no administrative powers, but was conceived solely as a research agency. It soon became the authoritative source of information about the welfare of children and families in the United States. However, the bill that created it did not pass without strong opposition in the Senate. Some argued that the bill was inspired by foreign socialists who wanted to use the agency to control the nation's children. There was also concern that the bureau would support child-labor legislation. Others feared that the powers of the states would be undermined by federal legislation. Other opponents worried about the autonomy of the family. Senator Heburn of Idaho thought the bill would implement the tyranny of Plato's Republic:

> This measure is not new. It is something after the character of the arrangement of the Greeks before our era, when the State was the nursery of the children; and they carried it to very great extremes. Finally, one crank, following in the footsteps of another, conceived the idea that the children should be so mixed and so reared that it would be impossible for any particular person or any particular child to recognize any particular person as its parent. . . . Is that the purpose? Are we going to start out to exploit the individual judgment and idiosyncrasies of parents at public expense? (quoted in Bremner 1970, 766–67)

The White House Conference in 1909 and the establishment of the Children's Bureau in 1912 are watersheds in American public policy toward children. Underneath all the compromises, they still represent the first time the federal government recognized and acknowledged the rights of children independent of their parents and sought to protect them.

The Children's Bureau had mixed success when it sought to expand its brief by sponsoring the 1921 Sheppard-Towner Act, the first federally funded healthcare program in the United States. Its agenda was to reduce infant and maternal mortality rates and to provide states with matching federal funds to establish childhealth centers. The program lasted until 1929, when, under the pressure of the American Medical Association, Congress refused to renew it.

All these developments reflected the idea that parents should be held responsible for the welfare of their children. Their failure to properly provide for their children was now a violation of public standards. The suffering child became the object of public concern framed by the newly defined responsibilities—or lack of responsibilities—of its parents. At the time, these new definitions arose with a relaxing of the state's punitive grip; the goal of saving families was much milder from a parent's point of view than the previous practice of taking children away. But decades later this qualitatively new definition of children as beings with rights would come into conflict with the priority of holding families together.

The Societies for the Prevention of Cruelty to Children gradually came to reflect the tendency of the times. They were less and less concerned with the prosecution of the offenders that was their original purpose; more and more they concentrated on family rehabilitation. In 1910, the secretary of the New York Society could still claim that "child rescue is not child reformation, it is not charitable work, it terrifies the cruel by the vigor of its prosecution" (American Humane Association 1910, 2). But a decade later, in its Forty-Fifth Annual Report, the New York Society expressed its goal as "the assistance and supervision of the Society in the rehabilitation of homes. . . . [E]very effort is made to save the children to their homes" (New York Society for the Prevention of Cruelty to Children 1920, 1). In 1922 there were more than three hundred such societies nationwide, and almost all followed these guidelines.

As practice changed, so did terminology. The term "cruelty" almost disappeared and was replaced by "neglect." This rhetorical change from the morally and emotionally highly charged term "cruelty" to the more diffuse term "neglect" reflects the change from heroic to routine intervention. But at the same time, precisely because it did not require actual malice, "neglect" was capable of taking on a broader and broader definition: failure of supervision, inappropriate clothing, inattention to physical needs, and moral negligence through sexual conduct in the presence of children were now all offenses. The child-welfare workers tried to teach immigrants the new standards of middle-class parenthood. Children had to be removed from dangerous streets; sleeping arrangements organized so that parents and children did not share the same bed, or even the same room; and both fathers and mothers were to stay home and not frequent the local saloons. Failure to meet these standards was defined as neglect.

Alcoholism was among the major factors in the neglect of children, and the fight against alcoholism became one of the central struggles against the immoral conduct of parents. Again, the new reformers took up a theme of the earlier generation, but understood it in a new way. T. H. Green formulated the problem of drunkenness as an impediment for the development of a democratic citizenry:

> Drunkenness in the head of the family means, as a rule, the impoverishment and degradation of all members of the family. . . . Here, then, is a wide-spreading social evil, of which society may, if it will, by a restraining law, to a great extent rid itself, to the infinite enhancement of the positive freedom enjoyed by its members. . . . But to argue that an effectual law in restraint of the drink-traffic would be a wrongful interference with individual liberty is to ignore the essential condition under which alone every particular liberty can rightly be allowed to the individual, the condition namely, that the allowance of that liberty is not, as a rule, and on the whole, an impediment to social good. (Green 1986, 210–11)

Campaigns against drinking can therefore be considered as part of the Progressive attempts to educate citizens in the virtues of self-respect, prudence, and industriousness, virtues of "ordinary citizens." To restrict drinking is certainly the exercise of control, but not control in the sense of restricting freedom. On the contrary, it is control in the name of the enhancement of freedom, namely positive freedom, the freedom for self-realization and self-development.

Children's rights were carved out against the rights of parents. Participants in an international conference on child welfare in 1918 formulated a "New Bill of Rights of Childhood." The participants agreed that every child has: a right to life; a right to a mother; a right to a home; a right to liberty; a right to play; a right to the pursuit of happiness (quoted in Hiner 1979, 239). To guarantee these rights was automatically to restrict the rights of parents to treat their children as the parents wished. Neglect expanded into areas that implied not only severe physical cruelty, but immorality, delinquency, and child labor. Public responsibility and regulation in the areas of children's delinquency and child labor were other major battlegrounds on which controversies regarding the distinctions between private and public authority were fought out. As with other reforms of this era, state policy was framed with the purpose of preserving, rather than eroding, the family. The restrictions of personal license that resulted were justified as necessary to secure the social conditions needed for the exercise of positive freedom. Private and public virtue were complementary. The moral order was conceived of as one in which all are called upon to participate—as the democratic life of society, which is the same as the life of society. And those who did not yet participate, such as immigrants and the poor, had to be brought in. Reeducation rather than retribution became the way to improve society.

THE JUVENILE COURT

This program of reeducation can be clearly seen in the way Progressive reformers treated juvenile criminals. Juvenile criminals were perceived as victims of neglect. The agenda was to prevent future crime by the turning of juvenile delinquents into future responsible citizens. Illinois established the first juvenile court in 1899. By 1925, every state except Maine and Wyoming had passed laws authorizing their establishment. The idea that guided these courts was that juvenile offenders were not to be treated as criminals, since no child was mature enough morally to be a criminal, but rather as victims of circumstance and parental failing. The legal rationale for this interference in the family was the principle of *parens patriae.* According to this doctrine of English common law, the king of England was responsible for all the children needing protection in his kingdom. This function passed from the king to the states and from the states to the courts. The juvenile judge was to be a substitute parental figure talking to the child in an informal setting. Judge Harvey Baker, the first judge of the Juvenile Court of Boston, explained:

The Boston Juvenile Court is administered on the assumption that the fundamental function of a Juvenile Court is to put each child who comes before it in a normal relation to society as promptly and as permanently as possible, and that while punishment is not by any means to be dispensed with, it is to be made subsidiary and subordinate to that function. The officials of the court believe it is helpful to think of themselves as physicians in a dispensary. . . . If the child denies the truth of the charge against him, the judge sometimes talks with him at considerable length, reasoning with him, but never threatening him or offending him or offering inducements to him directly or indirectly, or asking him to inform on other children unless they are much older than he. The child is told in the course of a free conversation between him and the judge that in this court there is only thing worse than stealing, and that is not telling the truth about it afterwards. (Baker 1910, 643)

The judge in this procedural change was to become the benevolent father the child lacked. Judge Ben Lindsey, the juvenile court judge of Denver, emphasized that "more is accomplished through love than by any other method" (quoted in Ryerson 1978, 39). Proponents of the juvenile court were very much influenced by the language of the Social Gospel. They emphasized that the capacity to love and to be loved could cross classes and ethnic groups. Lyman Abbott, in his *Christianity and Social Problems* (1896), addresses at length the question of how society should deal with criminals. His answer clearly rejects retributive justice and proposes the principle of love: "Our penal systems should be animated by a different spirit; they should seek a different end; they should employ a different means. The spirit should be that of love; the object should be the reformation of the offender" (311).

The court expanded the authority of legal, which is to say state, institutions. Its proponents and judges saw themselves as teachers of the downtrodden, the poor, and the immigrants. Judges taught children in their courts about punctuality, cleanliness, and other moral virtues. As Judge Lindsey put it: "I do not want only to teach children how and why they should obey the law but also to make them really patriotic in spirit, protectors of the state and upholders of its laws" (quoted in Ryerson 1978, 48). These reformers not only wanted to improve upon the criminal-justice system but to educate the children and their families into a life of middle-class respectability. This is why parents and children appeared in court together.

A key actor in this program of reform was the probation officer. Modeled after the "friendly visitor" of the Charity Organization Society, the probation officer entered the delinquent child's household as a friend of the family. Members of the National Congress of Mothers, a woman's organization founded in 1897 with the goal of promoting the ideals of an educated motherhood, were among the most enthusiastic volunteers. They saw an opportunity to influence directly the lower classes and immigrants in the virtues of good parenting. The ideal probation officer had no simple task with the child in his or her charge: "There is such a thing as an instantaneous awakening of the soul to the realization of higher and better things by the magnetic influence of one soul reacting upon the other" (quoted in Rothman 1978, 52). This is of course much more than exercising control over poor and immigrant parents and their children. Interaction between lower-class parents and their "betters" was to transform the family in the image of the reformer. As Homer Folks explained the purpose of probation:

> Probation has to do with moral delinquency. As applied to neglected children it is, in effect, an effort to reach the parents, and to affect, for good, their attitude toward their children. It implies, in substance, a conviction. . . . It is the personal influence of the probation officer, going into the child's home, studying the surroundings and influences that are shaping the child's career, discovering the processes which have been exercising an unwholesome influence, and so far as possible, remedying these conditions, this is the very essence of the probation system. The friendly side of the probation officer's work is its important side. His duty is by no means simply that of securing information for the court as to the child's conduct, but that of securing reformation. He is not to be a dispassionate observer but an active influence. (quoted in Bremner 1970, 530)

The juvenile-court system combined the adversarial proceedings of criminal procedure with the understanding of judges and probation officers for the life circumstances of the offenders. Judge Charles Heuisler, the Juvenile Court judge of Baltimore, emphasized, "Homes must be re-created, not repressed. The work of children's courts must be done in the children's homes. The voice of pity and compassion must reach him in his home, and reach parents in his home" (Heuisler 1903, 301).

After a decade of existence, the court became the subject of critical investigations. Suits were filed against the court on constitutional grounds, claiming that it violated the rights of parents. Also, within the system, confidence in the rehabilitation of juvenile offenders was seriously questioned. Furthermore, the use of volunteer probation officers came under more scrutiny. Professional social workers especially expressed their dissatisfaction with the methods and organization of the work of the courts. They attacked the system of probation officers' recruitment. These volunteers had largely been recruited from churches, with no attention paid to training. There was growing demand for paid probation officers with social-work training. Almost all connected with the juvenile court discovered that "compassion" could hardly be administered by a court of law. Even the maxim of family preservation could not be upheld; more and more, courts removed children from their homes and committed them to institutions.

Judge Baker, one of the most enthusiastic judges of the court, expressed his disappointment in 1920:

> The reasons for this failure [of the juvenile court system] are many. Among them are poorly conceived laws, inadequate equipment both personal and material, and incompetent judges; but by far the most salient reason is that courts are not funda-

mentally adapted to this work. . . . The true function of a court is to determine judicially the facts at issue before it. . . . Investigations into the lives, environments, or heredity of delinquents, the infliction of punishment and the supervision of probation . . . are repugnant to every tenet of the science of law. (quoted in Ryerson 1978, 141)

As a consequence, most rehabilitative functions of the court were transferred to public schools or to psychiatric clinics established for the purpose of giving psychological help to offenders. One of the best known examples is the Judge Baker Guidance Center, founded in Boston in 1917. By 1922, there were forty-two such clinics in the United States. Moral rehabilitation was transformed into therapy, as the relationship between officials and clients was redefined from "friendship" to a therapeutic stance. Juvenile delinquents were referred to these clinics by judges, so that the punitive and rehabilitative work could be separated. Social workers, mostly trained in psychiatry, tried to treat children and their parents, teaching mothers guidelines of child care and advising fathers not to treat their children brutally. Most of the children's problems were blamed on the parents, mothers in particular, but the case studies of these clinics demonstrate that the social workers were sympathetic to parents and tried to teach them "good parenting." The establishment of guidance clinics made it possible to leave rehabilitation to trained specialists, after court proceedings were completed.

THE CAMPAIGN AGAINST CHILD LABOR

Between 1870 and 1930, a battle was fought to remove children from the labor force. The 1890 census showed that more than 1.5 million children between ages ten and fifteen were gainfully employed, more than 18 percent of all the children in that age group. The 1900 census increased that number by a quarter million. Children under ten were not even recorded, so a rough estimate would place 2 million children under age fifteen in the coal mines and factories of 1900. But by 1930, most of those were removed from the labor force and put into schools.

The industrial revolution did not create child labor—children have always worked—but it vastly expanded the opportunities for their employment. This was a particular problem in the South. Irene Ashby, a representative of the American Federation of Labor, conducted the first extensive investigation of cotton mills in Alabama in 1901, and it was in Alabama that the first state Child Labor Committee was founded by the clergyman Edgar Gardner Murphy. One year later, the New York Child Labor Committee came into existence. It was composed of social workers, reformers, and academicians. Its most prominent members were Florence Kelley, the secretary of the National Consumers' League, and Felix Adler, the secretary of the Ethical Culture Society in New York. Florence Kelley's *Some Ethical Gains through Legislation* (1905) applied the principles of ethical democracy to the question of child labor; the right to a decent childhood, and the fulfillment of childhood's potential, were basic goals for the realization of democracy:

[T]he right to childhood exists. [It] follows from the existence of the Republic and must be guarded in order to guard its life which must perish if it should ever cease to be replenished by generation of patriots, who can be secured on no other terms than the full recognition of the need of long-cherished, carefully nurtured childhood for all the future citizens. (3)

Murphy and members of the New York Committee worked on the organization of a national committee, which was founded on April 15, 1904. Adler expressed the need for a national body:

It shall be a great moral force for the protection of children. It is to combat the danger in which childhood is placed by greed and rapacity. . . . It should be plainly said that whatever happens in the sacrifice of adult workers, the public conscience inexorably demands that the children under twelve years of age shall not be touched; that childhood shall be sacred; that industrialism and commercialism shall not be allowed beyond this point to degrade humanity. This function of the Committee will be a preventive one. By no other means than those that have been suggested can the needless sacrifice of child life be prevented. (quoted in Trattner 1970, 58–59)

National magazines and popular books took up the question of child labor. Advocates of child-labor regulation used the term "child slavery" and exposed it as cruel and harsh.

The National Child Labor Committee (NCLC) was one of the first organizations to take up the crusade against child labor. It started out by gathering data and supplying it to social scientists, who published their findings in the *Annals of the American Academy of Political and Social Sciences*. In its first year, the NCLC distributed 48,500 pamphlets and some 35,000 pieces of literature. The committee also founded its own journal, *Child Labor Bulletin*, which reported routinely on its activities and legislative gains. Together with the Children's Bureau, the NCLC tried to push federal legislation concerning child labor. It met with modest success. Several states did pass laws regulating child labor, but they were unevenly enforced. The passage of the Keating-Owing Act in 1916 was considered their main triumph:

Be it enacted by the Senate and the House of Representatives of the United States of America in Congress assembled, That no producer, manufacturer, or dealer shall ship or deliver for shipment in interstate or foreign commerce any article or commodity the product of any mine or quarry, situated in the United States, in which within thirty days prior to the time of the removal of such product therefrom children under the age of sixteen years have been employed or permitted to work. (quoted in Bremner 1970, 703)

But the law was immediately challenged on constitutional grounds. The Committee of Southern Manufacturers was founded in 1915 with the express purpose of opposing all attempts to extend federal legislation. It lobbied Congress and the Supreme Court against the legislation, and in 1918, in *Hammer v. Dagenhart,* the U.S. Supreme Court declared the act unconstitutional on the grounds that it exceeded the constitutional authority of Congress over the states. The attempt to push a Child Labor Amendment, which was supported by the NCLC and the American Federation of Labor, failed in 1924. One opposing voice was raised by the Woman Patriot Publishing Company, an anti–women's suffrage organization: "The youthful poor of the Nation, if forbidden to work up to 18 by the Government, with the alternative of obeying the law or of starving, would be driven to work underground . . ." (quoted in Bremner 1970, 735). Opponents also used Florence Kelley's socialist leanings to demonstrate that federal child-labor legislation was a Communist plot organized by Moscow. Thus, one of the manufacturers' journals, the *Manufacturers' Record,* published the following account in 1924:

This proposed amendment is fathered by Socialists, Communists and Bolshevists. They are the active workers in its favor. They look forward to its adoption as giving them the power to nationalize the children of the land and bring about in this country the exact conditions which prevail in Russia. . . . If adopted, this amendment would be the greatest thing ever done in America in behalf of the activities of Hell. It would make millions of young people under 18 years of age idlers in brain and body, and thus make them the devil's best workshop. It would destroy the initiative and self-reliance and manhood and womanhood of all the coming generations. (*Manufacturers' Record* 1924)

Defenders of child-labor legislation argued that, on the contrary, the right to an uneconomical childhood would be the only guarantee for the future of the American democracy.

Fierce opposition against child-labor regulation did not come only from laissez-faire advocates and "negative" liberals. Strong opposition came from parents, who were often dependent on the income of their children for their own household economy. Mostly immigrants, coming from agrarian backgrounds, these parents were strongly committed to a conception of childhood in which children contributed economically to the household. Zelizer (1985) stresses this aspect of child-labor regulation and demonstrates how reformers tried to universalize their conceptions of an "emotionally priceless" child against the resistance of poor and immigrant parents. Spargo (1906) echoes this sentiment:

There is the senseless, feverish, natural ambition of the immigrant to save money. . . . How often I have heard that speech! Not always in the broken music of Italian-English, but in the many-toned, curious English of Bohemian, Lithuanian, Scandinavian, Russian, Pole, and Greek—all drawn by the same powerful magnet of wealth—all sacrificing, ignorantly and blindly, the lives of themselves and their children in their fevered quest. . . . If the nation is to receive these immigrants, the nation must accept the responsibility of protecting them and itself. (214)

But more than the normative struggle between two different family economies was at stake. There was cultural disagreement over the economic and sentimental value of children. But child-labor regulations also reflected the admittance of children into the arena of public concern; it treated them as present and future citizens who share in the universal human nature that underlies civic equality. It is this conception that legitimized intrusions on parental authority and the right of contract. Civic equality for children did not mean that they were able to enter into contracts with employers, nor were their parents allowed to do so on their behalf. For true, as opposed to formal, democracy to succeed, education is indispensable. Child labor, like child delinquency, is an impediment to this goal. Child-labor regulations and compulsory education are therefore two sides of the same coin. Removed from the factories, put into schools, children were supposed to learn one language and one code of conduct, conducive to the public ethos of the nation.

THE GENERALIZATION OF INTERDEPENDENCE

Compassion was no longer directed solely to the immediate neighbor, but through the aid of legislation and standardized forms of correct child-rearing, extended to strangers as well. This "generalization of interdependence" is a feature of democratization. Compassion toward children in the beginning of the twentieth century underwent such a generalization of interdependence. Mothers' pensions to help children remain at home; probation officers of juvenile courts, first volunteers, then paid social workers administering to the needs of troubled children; and finally, the most generalized and abstract measure of all, the removal of children from factories were all moments in this development.

During this period, child neglect became a clearly defined crime. Juvenile courts did not only deal with child offenders, but also brought parents before judges, when referred by either anticruelty societies or other charity organizations. In that respect the court clearly interfered in the family life of the parents, in order either to establish conditions that did not constitute neglect or to remove the child from the family. With all its faults, the juvenile-court movement established a principle of public compassion in a somewhat bureaucratized form. Thousands of neglected children were in dire need of public intervention into the privacy of the family. A Russian father, appearing before the juvenile court in Los Angeles, declared to the judge, "Oh, Fred! . . . He is wicked. I beat him to death, then they say, it is against the law." The juvenile court, even though it failed often to live up to its own standards, affirmed the responsibility of the state to every child within its citizenry, the meaning of *parens patriae*. It was an acknowledgment that children are not only part of the social system, but because they are the future citizens of the state, the state bears a special responsibility toward them.

Anthony Platt (1977), in a by now classic study on the emergence of the juvenile court, has argued that the reformers of the juvenile court were not motivated by a desire to foster the welfare of children, but by their urge to control the children of the working classes. He claims that the expansion of their authority disqualifies them from being called "humanitarians." However, the dichotomy between "humanitarianism" and "control" is false. To be humane, or to be compassionate, does not mean to have less control over one's fellow citizens. Lasch claims that "bourgeois domesticity was imposed on society by the forces of organized virtue, led by feminists, temperance advocates, educational reformers, liberal ministers, penologists, and bureaucrats" (1977, 169). But Gordon (1988) has convincingly demonstrated that very often the "imposed upon" came to the agencies themselves and asked for direct interference. Older children complained about their brutal fathers, mothers about neglectful husbands, and so on. These "bourgeois virtues" were not rejected by the clients as much as they are by modern-day theorists speaking in their place.

Whatever the motivation of reformers, the lives of children became the object of the "dispassionate compassion" of state institutions. The understanding the juvenile-court reformers had of humanitarianism and compassion was one of corrective discipline. The ideal society they aimed at was one in which citizenship would transcend ethnicity and class. Not the "domestication" of the poor, but their "civilization"—their education in the manners essential to democracy—was the agenda not so hidden behind the instilling of parental responsibility toward their children. Compassion without control, without asking for anything in return, is the Catholic idea of compassion, modeled on the saints, who were in turn supposed to be mirroring God's image in their boundless love for all they encountered in mankind. But the public compassion of the state is a compassion that demands a return, namely the moralization of the recipients. It is no less compassionate for that; rather it is a different form of compassion, one that does not depend on individual heroics. Compassion and control are reconciled in the concept of positive freedom. The state was responsible for socializing its citizens.

Thus, the generalization of interdependence and the transition from the "friendly visitor" to abstract laws and entitlement did not diminish the moral agenda underlying these reforms. As insufficient as these measures were from a later historical stance, they were developments in the formation of public compassion and responsibility. The predicament these Progressive reformers tried to solve was the harmonization of liberal individualism and the free market with the principles of citizenship and civic solidarity. This predicament was expressed theoretically by thinkers like Green and Dewey, and expressed practically by the reform of children's lives. Children were the unwilling mediators between these two principles.

Chapter 5

The Universalization of Compassion

We have seen that in the second half of the nineteenth century, there was an organized attempt to wipe out cruelty to children. "Cruel" people are by definition bad people, and the crusade against cruelty was understood primarily as a moral crusade. It is true that some kinds of cruelty, such as working children to death, were understood to be systematic, and were dealt with through the state, through the passage of anti–child-labor laws. But in general, such systematic explanations were subordinated to the vocabulary of moral uplift. In addition, the class components of the crusade were fairly stark. Middle-class reformers, many of them religiously inspired, chiefly aimed their efforts at working-class children. Underlying this was a fairly clear understanding of the interaction of "environment" with moral failure: poverty caused depravity as often as depravity caused poverty. But none of these social understandings changed the moral focus. The reformers were trying to save the children from the depravity into which they were born and into which, without help, they would fall themselves.

The "cruelty against children" of the nineteenth century eventually became the "child abuse" of today. The Societies for the Prevention of Cruelty to Children eventually became the child-welfare agencies of the modern state. This chapter is the story of that transformation. Cruelty is an individual, moral quality of adults. Child abuse, on the other hand, is a violation of rights. In classical political thought concerned with "rights," children were never granted any rights. Therefore, the process of defining and enforcing those rights produces paradoxes and aporias.

Furthermore, although the underlying moral thrust of modern child advocacy is similar in many ways to that of Victorian reformers, the vocabulary has shifted from moral to scientific. The class-based moral vocabulary that legitimated state action then is insufficient to legitimate state action now, if it is not actually de-delegitimating. Victorians thought that the "better" classes should set an example for the "lower" classes, that such behavior was a duty, a moral action.

Nowadays, the more a social movement appears to be one class's attempt to impose its will on another, the less it can claim the moral high ground. The tensions between the moral impulse of reform, the democratic censure on the vocabulary of class, and the need for "expert" knowledge to legitimate state programs have all combined to change not only the discourse but also the practice of preventing child abuse. And one of the more striking results has been the shift in focus from the nineteenth-century emphasis on physical cruelty (with a secondary disgust with sexual laxness) to the current emphasis on sexual abuse. The beating of children still counts, of course, as child abuse. But the central referent of the term "child abuse," the first aspect that comes to mind, is its sexual referent. And this, I will show, is in large part because the sexual abuse of children does not exhibit the clear correlation with class that corporal abuse does, and it was therefore better suited as the main exhibit in the halls of Congress during the formative period of institutionalization.

THE BUREAUCRATIZATION OF COMPASSION

From the beginning of the twentieth century to the 1960s, anticruelty activism declined, as did volunteer activism on behalf of children. Many believed that the former agitation which had resulted in child-protection legislation had extinguished "cruelty" to children. Compassion underwent bureaucratization, and the heroic age of the volunteer gave way to public administration. Private philanthropy was replaced by the medical profession and social workers. The decades before the 1950s reflected a rather low public awareness of the problems of children (Gordon 1988, 158–67). New concepts replaced "cruelty," which was transformed into "emotional neglect," informed by a Freudian rhetoric. "Emotional neglect," a concept not limited to lower-class people or immigrants, replaced the earlier concept of "cruelty" and "moral neglect," becoming the standard diagnosis used by child-protection agencies. The journal *Social Work* used the term in the 1950s as the most common category of child mistreatment (Gordon 1988, 345). It usually pointed to inadequate attachment between mothers and children, taking love between mothers and children for granted. Most child-development researchers at the time prescribed motherly care as the most important element in child rearing and warned that neglect of these motherly duties would lead to grave emotional consequences for the child.

The stance toward perpetrators changed from a moral to a therapeutic one, characterized by rational and abstract language. Whereas half a century earlier, child-welfare reformers believed that material aid in the form of mothers' pensions would cure the problem of neglect (Leff 1973), emotional neglect could only be treated by therapeutic intervention. Freudian ideas put the moral and legal responsibility of parents (especially mothers) in question through the privatization of its moral language. This also led to a transformation of public compassion into a form of sentimentalized pity toward victims and perpetrators alike. These understandings diminished the legal prosecution of child cruelty so prevalent in the early phases of child protection.

Concern with these matters reappeared in the 1960s, largely redefined in terms of "child abuse." Concern with "child abuse" reappeared at the same time minorities struggled for equal rights. In the language of child advocates, suffering children became one more "minority." This very redefinition of children as a "minority" is indicative of the new understanding of compassion at this time. Before, suffering children were compared with suffering animals, evoking compassion for defenseless suffering. The concept of "child as suffering minority" evoked a legal and political understanding based on universal rights. A children's-liberation movement, though smaller in scope and less significant than other "rights" movements, demanded equal rights for children (Margolin 1978). The movement challenged the achievements of earlier generations as "patronizing" children. Child protection was challenged as being child oppression in the name of government intervention and total parental power over the child. Furthermore, it was suggested that children should have the right to work, the right to sexual freedom, etc. (Farson 1974).

In 1959, the United Nations General Assembly unanimously passed a Declaration of the Rights of the Child. It focused on nutrition, housing, recreation, medical service, education, and protection from neglect and exploitation. Discrimination based on age joined other discriminations and joined ranks with sexism and racism. The universal character of this declaration is expressed in its preamble: "Mankind owes to the child the best it has to give" (United Nations 1960, 19).

THE RIGHTS REVOLUTION

This points to an expansion of democracy in recognizing children's needs and interests not as duties of adults to uphold but as rights under law. This is of course inconsistent with earlier understandings that rights cannot be granted to those in dependency relations. Children are not able to take care of themselves and are therefore dependent on others. Compassion and consequent legalization of child protection did not grant rights to children, rather the opposite, as the juvenile court deprived children in the name of a special protective relationship of the constitutional right of due process (Ryerson 1978; Schlossman 1977). This was changed in 1967, when the Supreme Court in *De Gault* provided children in juvenile courts the rights of due process like those of adults. On the other hand, the Supreme Court upheld the right of schoolteachers to beat children, and denied in *Ingraham v. Wright* (1977) that beatings in schools constituted "cruel and unusual punishment" (Hyman 1990, 52–54). Discussions about political, sexual, and other rights of children were held on a rather high theoretical level, but in the end the phrase "children's rights" became "a slogan in search of a definition." (Rodham 1973, 487; see also Franklin 1988 and Wringe 1981). Without a group claiming these rights for itself, compassion for children had to concentrate on restricting the rights of the caretakers of children rather than investing children themselves with such rights. There is also a certain irony involved. Children are victimized because they are powerless, yet very often the legal response to their victimization relies on children's capacity to testify in court. Child victims must undergo the same legal processes as those imposed on adult victims (Myers 1985; Thomas 1972).

Children's-rights activism also never developed the moral fervor of parallel developments in the "animal rights" movement. After World War II, several animal-welfare movements became more vocal (Jasper and Nelkin 1992). A growing movement developed, again adding the language of "rights" to its struggle against cruelty. Like other contemporary movements, it was inspired by a criticism of modern instrumentalism. Groups like the Animal Liberation Front, founded in 1979, broke into laboratories conducting animal research and freed the animals. That humans are superior to other species is "speciesism," with the understanding that animals suffer injustice like other oppressed groups. This development was facilitated because there were no privacy rights for the caretakers of animals, making it easier for activists to "interfere" in the lives of animals than in those of children.

THE DUTY TO RESCUE

Before 1962, legislation did not require the reporting of battered children. Between 1963 and 1967, every state passed some form of child-abuse reporting law, requiring professionals who come in contact with children to report their suspected abuse (Nelson 1984, 76ff). Reporting laws are especially interesting for the study of public moral sentiments like compassion, since they constitute a partial break with the Anglo-Saxon common-law tradition of the legal duty to be compassionate. Anglo-Saxon common law does not compel active benevolence among human beings. Although child-abuse reporting laws are restricted to professionals, they mandate a duty to prevent harm. Laws that require citizens to prevent harm, usually called "duty to rescue" or "Good Samaritan" laws, have been part of almost all of the civic codes of Continental legal traditions since the mid–nineteenth century (Feinberg 1984; Kirchheimer 1942; Kleinig 1976; Lipkin 1983; Rosenberg 1985). However, the Anglo-Saxon legal tradition does not recognize a duty to come to the aid of strangers in distress. The legitimacy of reporting laws in the United States has been debated by legal scholars because in this case the law requires a "duty to rescue." One of the earliest suggestions to change the law in America was proposed in 1908 by James Ames, who wrote:

One who fails to interfere to save another from impending death or great bodily harm, when he might do so with little or no inconvenience to himself, and death or great bodily harm follows as a consequence of his inaction, shall be punished criminally. (Ames 1908, 113)

Most suggestions to change the law rest on Ames's proposal, and only Vermont in the 1970s and Minnesota in the 1980s put "easy rescue" legislation on their books.

Most of the opponents of such legislation on moral grounds argue that the "duty to rescue" deprives the individual of his or her liberty to choose whether to rescue the endangered victim. By this, the state deprives individuals of their capacity to make moral choices through mandating them by law. In societies in which the idea of public compassion has not influenced policy to the extent it has in the Anglo-American countries, the state has assumed the duty to regulate moral conduct earlier exercised by the church. This explains partially the predominance of "duty to rescue" laws on the Continent. In societies, on the other hand, in which policy has been influenced by ideals of compassion, persons owe moral duties directly to each other, without the state's mediation. The state in this tradition is not constitutive of moral obligation, but creates conditions in which people can effectively exercise moral obligations between them. Therefore, child-abuse reporting laws require intervention not of all of the public, but only of those experts who come into contact with children. Child-abuse reporting laws were the first attempt in the United States to legislate compassion for children from those professionals who come in daily contact with them. Civil immunity is granted to those reporting in good faith, and most provisions also waive the spousal and physician–patient privileges in such cases (Davis and Schwartz 1987, 167–69).

THE CREATION OF FORMAL KNOWLEDGE

However, no clear definitions of child abuse were in place, which in turn limited the capacity of outsiders to interfere (Besharov 1990). It seems clear at the outset that the broader the definition of child abuse, the greater the extent of child abuse. Child abuse has been defined as "nonaccidental physical attack or physical injury, including minimal as well as fatal injury, inflicted upon children by persons caring for them"; or as "inflicted gaps or deficits between circumstances of being which would facilitate the optimal development of children to which they should be entitled, and their actual circumstances, irrespective of the cause of deficit" (Hacking 1991, 270–71).

Both definitions were created by one of the most outspoken defenders of children's rights in the United States, David Gil. Whereas the first speaks about very concrete acts, the second defines the undefinable, namely "gaps between the optimal and the actual," the optimal being undefined. When child abuse is defined as preventing the "optimal" development of children, the definition so becomes vaguely and massively inclusive.

National legislation, the Child Abuse Prevention Act, was put into place in 1974. The act established a National Center on Child Abuse and Neglect, to provide, among other things, for financial assistance to be given to a demonstration program for the prevention, identification, and treatment of child abuse and neglect. The definition, worked out in Senate hearings, was this:

> "child abuse and neglect" means the physical or mental injury, sexual abuse or exploitation, negligent treatment, or maltreatment of a child . . . under circumstances which indicate that the child's health or welfare is harmed or threatened thereby. (U.S. Senate 1973)

Gil emphasized the broadness of this definition to demonstrate the prevalence of abuse. When he sought to show that child abuse was more common among the poor, he was immediately contradicted by Senator Mondale: "But this is not a poverty problem; it is a national problem" (U.S. Senate 1973, 17). This remark reflected then-current attempts by professionals and the public alike to dissociate the problems of child abuse from those of poverty. Indeed, at least in the public perception, as well as in policy making, child abuse became universalized. In contrast to the "heroic" age of anticruelty drives, the poor were not perceived as a separate moral entity. Everybody abuses children. Political tactics might also have played a role. The public was disenchanted with the "war on poverty" of the 1960s, and President Nixon was poised to veto all antipoverty legislation. In 1971, Mondale tried to pass the Comprehensive Child Development Act, providing for the expansion of children's services, especially of daycare. President Nixon vetoed it, commenting that it would "commit the vast moral authority of the National Government to the side of communal approaches to child rearing over the family approach" (quoted in Grubb and Lazerson 1982, 214). (In 1976, Senator Mondale and Congressman Brademas tried to sponsor the Comprehensive Child and Family Services Act, which was defeated as well.) In the political climate of 1974, with its focus on the purported classlessness of child abuse and family centeredness, the legislation described above facilitated passage of the Child Abuse Prevention Act. As Mondale put it, "not even Richard Nixon is in favor of child abuse" (quoted in Nelson 1984, 102).

The struggle to pass federal child-abuse legislation also reflects deeper political and ideological struggles. A central conflict between liberalism and conservatism since the 1960s has centered on the extension of constitutional rights to previously disenfranchised and marginal groups like homosexuals, criminals, women, even animals (Edsall and Edsall 1990). Especially in the courts, an expansive drive by a range of civil-liberties organizations fought for new rights for recreational drug users, the mentally ill, gays, American Indians, illegal aliens, the dependent poor, criminal defendants, and prisoners, marking the period as a "rights revolution" (Walker 1990, 299–320). Millions of people—students, prisoners, women, the poor, gays and lesbians, the handicapped, the mentally retarded—voiced demands for rights. So, for instance, the American Civil Liberties Union succeeded in the *King v. Smith* decision of 1971 in invalidating rules that denied Aid to Families with Dependent Children (AFDC) benefit payments to children whose mothers lived with someone to whom the mothers were not married. This decision made AFDC payments available to an estimated five hundred thousand previously ineligible children. In this era, "compassion" has become a routine rhetorical term in American politics. Rather than being the consequence of compassionate policies, the "rights revolution" is a consequence of contending political forces. However, the term "compassion" was used consistently in this connection. These factors contributed to a conservative backlash and to an increased discrediting of "liberal" compassion. As Samuel Walker, the historian of the ACLU, observed, "a rights consciousness permeated society in the mid-1970s" (1990, 320), and to a great extent the conservative revolt against rights was a reaction against the civil-liberties gains of the previous decade. Especially, the emphasis of the "rights revolution" on "negative" freedoms—freedom from authority, from repression, etc.—made the commitment to an entity larger than the self, such as family or country, look like "traditional" values, which became part of the conservative struggle against liberalism in America.

Federal legislation seeking to detect child abuse positioned the federal government to assume an active role in its prevention, detection, and treatment. There was and is considerable confusion over the definition of child abuse, and none has been officially adopted. The medical, legal, and social-service professions developed their own criteria, which in turn differ from those of the public. Nonetheless, the 1974 act clearly demonstrated legalized public compassion toward children, even in the very vagueness of its terminology, of which "mental suffering" and "endangering health" are representative (see Giovannoni and Becarra 1979 on the different dimensions of the definition of child abuse).

That the concept of compassion became more universal—less linked to poverty and to differing cultural patterns—is expressed in the professionalization of the language addressing children's suffering. In 1962 a group of Denver pediatricians, led by C. H. Kempe, published the article "The Battered-Child Syndrome" in the prestigious *Journal of the American Medical Association.* This study drew attention to persistent and repeated injuries to small children, using X rays as evidence. The doctors talked about a "syndrome" caused by parents' beating of children. This was not the first time that doctors pointed to this phenomenon. In France, around the end of the nineteenth and beginning of the twentieth centuries, several French doctors and legal–medical scholars pointed to the prevalence of physical and sexual abuse of children, calling the phenomenon *"attentats aux moeurs,"* an attack on public morality (Bernard 1886; Brouardel 1909; Lacassagne 1886; Tardieu 1878).

Medical specialists were not, as such, involved in the earlier American child-saving movements, at a time when philanthropic work was not part of medicine (Hacking 1991, 265). In America, doctors paid attention to the willful infliction of injuries for the first time in the 1940s but did not explicitly say so, and nobody outside the medical profession paid much attention to it (Caffey 1946; see also Nelson 1984, 12). There was some agitation over child neglect in the 1950s, initiated by Vincent de Francis, the head of the Children's Division of the American Humane Association, but again without drawing much public attention (Pleck 1987, 164–67). With the publication of the Kempe article, matters changed. The media embraced the issue, and "child abuse" as a social problem was re-created. *Time* and *Newsweek* summarized the findings of the article, and television programs reported on the new "disease" (Nelson 1984, 56–75).

Child abuse conceived of as a disease provides a basis for universalized sympathy. Diseases may afflict everyone, not only the poor or culturally marginal. That all those afflicted by disease merit compassion is not a claim always recognized—witness AIDS in the current setting—but certainly the medical interpretation of child abuse widens the scope of public compassion. The "medicalization" of child abuse led other professions to join the systematization and rationalization of its discourse, including sociology.

Sociology was a latecomer to systematic research on child abuse. No sociological studies on the subject were published until the early 1970s, ten years after the beginning of modern research on child abuse. Between 1962 and 1972 the new subject was dominated by medical and psychological research. Doctors and psychologists defined the terms and set the agenda for social workers and state agencies. Sociologists found an established vocabulary and therapy and used it, formulating their research around the etiology, incidence, prevention, and treatment of child abuse.

These professional models regarding child abuse have been largely unquestioned. They hold that child abuse is cyclical, abused children becoming child abusers themselves. The task of prevention therefore is to break the cycle of abuse. Child abuse is a classless disease. Parents who beat their children were considered by authors specializing in the "battered-child syndrome" to suffer from severe emotional problems, defective character structure, poor emotional control, pervasive anger, psychosomatic illnesses, and a perverse fascination with punishment of children (for critics of this approach, see Gelles 1973 and Pelton 1989). Some of the basic texts explaining these factors to child-protective workers are mired in thick psychological jargon. Thus, Brandt Steele, author of many textbook articles on child abuse, writes:

> On a deeper psychological level, the events [of child abuse] begin with the parent's identification of the cared-for infant as a need-gratifying object equivalent to a parent who will replace the lacks in the abusive parent's own being-parented experience. Since the parent's past tells him that those to whom he looked for love were also the ones who attacked him, the infant is also perceived as a critical father figure. . . . A shift in identification occurs. The superego identification with the parent's own punitive parent takes over. The infant is perceived as the parent's own bad childhood itself. The built-up aggression is redirected outward, and the infant is hit with full superego approval. (Steele 1987, 90)

Although sharing some of its assumptions, sociological models rejected some of the medical etiology but operated within the same set of terms. Instead of medical and psychological factors, social and sociocultural causes were sought. All of the sociological approaches deal with the etiology of child abuse in a presentist mode. Sociological models such as resource theory, general systems theory, exchange theory, and others are used to explain the etiology of child abuse (Breines and Gordon 1983; Gelles 1985). Critics of the medical approach accuse doctors of blaming individuals, whereas sociologists would rather blame "society." A further attempt to frame the issue of child abuse not along moral but rather along rational and "amoral" lines is the sociological framework of the "sociology of deviance" and its application to child abuse. These studies attempt to locate the social forces that gave rise to the deviant labeling of child abusers (Gelles 1975).

UNIVERSALIZATION AND DEMORALIZATION

As a result of Progressive reforms, small children have become increasingly invisible in streets, working places, and other public arenas (Zelizer 1985). Their retreat into the privacy of homes made their treatment a problem of emotional management, and the corresponding mistreatment a disturbance in the same emotional management (Swaan 1981). Violent conduct in public places has been largely delegitimized among the urban middle and upper classes, and violence toward children is mediated through reports of professionals and the media as a problem of "intimate violence," as the term itself expresses. Reactions to urban violence by youngsters in poor neighborhoods recall the fears of urban disorder of the middle and late nineteenth century. The typical family is shielded from outsiders in emotional as well as spatial terms, allowing a large degree of privacy and seclusion. The professional syndrome regarded violence to children in such an enclosed setting as a breakdown in the management of intimate relations.

A casual look at newspapers and television programs over the last two decades reveals that child abuse of physical and emotional dimensions has been reported in unprecedented numbers as victims and aggressors, children and adults have taken their cases to the public. Watching the pictures of battered babies and children, listening to the litanies of evil that children recount, realizing the horrors and inhumanities that adults commit against children triggered a renewed surge of public compassion toward children. People were presented with parents who used cigarettes to burn children's skin, spilled boiling water over them, locked them up in dark rooms for days without food; in short, the violence of which totalitarian regimes are accused toward their citizens was revealed as the practice of daily life in many households under the regime of the private family in liberal society. The idyll of the family and of intimate relationships between parents and children is for many the key to civil society: an intimate realm in which caring will serve as a relief from the demands of an outside cruel world, a "haven in a

heartless world" (in the phrasing of Lasch 1977). Tortured children were the re-
minders that this project is a cruel irony for those whose torture chamber is the
household.

In whatever ways the concept of "child abuse" has been studied by professional
experts and by the media, the public has been socialized into perceiving violence
against children as a part of modern life. A new knowledge has been created.
Children are still treated arbitrarily: the "contract" between them and their parents is still not one of equals, but perhaps something new has been introduced.
The public is on notice that the parent–child or adult–child relationship poses
dangers to children's lives and safety. Children seem to be part of a generalized
network of interdependence. When a child is systematically hurt, "we" agree that
"somebody" should do something about it. That "somebody" becomes increasingly collective, the state.

CONSEQUENCES OF UNIVERSALIZATION

Assistance to the poor developed out of the tension between a perceived threat
to social order from the poor and the desire to preserve them as a future potential for productive labor. Different collectivities have dealt differently with the
poor over the course of time, the collectivity gradually enlarging and the poor
becoming more and more anonymous to the one providing the assistance. The
protection of children followed a similar path. Until the twentieth century, social policies directed toward children were embedded largely within the social
policy toward the poor. Children were therefore considered threats before they
were considered victims. In modern debates the poor are still partly seen as a
threat to the civil order and partly as victims of that very order, and public welfare
policies regarding them are informed by these two principles.

The perception of children as threats to an ordered and universal society is still
seen in the psychological theories of child abuse claiming that child abuse will
result in traumas and personality traits that when untreated will lead to future
abuse of the abused children's children. The cycle of poverty is reproduced in
the cycle of child abuse.

The earlier association between unacceptable treatment of children and poverty, or the problem of the "dangerous classes," disappeared: "experts" in "child
abuse," and political figures concerned with the cause, insist on the universality
of the problem in all classes and groups and that it can no longer be seen as the
unique failing of those laboring poor. It seems to be embarrassing for liberals to
locate the incidence of child abuse disproportionally among the poor, a scruple
that reformers in the last centuries had hardly developed (see Pelton 1978 for
criticism on the "classless" approach). This is another expression of how compassion has become universally inclusive. The poor, in the process of universalization, cannot be regarded as a separate entity anymore, capable of cruel conduct that others are not.

Following legislation and professionalization, public concern about children's safety has never been more expansive. Experts from all professions express their concern and give advice for help. More government agencies than ever deal with the plight of children. The expansion of compassion has reached unprecedented limits.

SEXUAL ABUSE AS CHILD ABUSE

A change in focus from "child abuse" to "sexual child abuse" occurred in the 1970s, initiated in part by the feminist movement. From the mid-1970s on, child abuse has often been identified completely with sexual abuse, and with this the definition of "abuse" has once again become very specific and narrow. A central issue here is that of "sexual child abuse" and of incest, defined as sexual child abuse in the family. Before this, sexual child abuse and child abuse were discussed separately; they are now joined in the contemporary professional literature.

Historically, sexual child abuse was discussed in France and in Germany-Austria among legal–medical professionals and later among psychoanalysts as a general concern of modern times. Wrote the famous scholar of sexual perversions Krafft-Ebing in 1895, "One of the most distressing phenomena of modern society is the increase of sexual crimes perpetrated by adults toward children" (see also Casper 1863). German scholars called these crimes *"Sittlichkeits verbrechen,"* the same term French scholars used, namely *attentats aux moeurs*; both terms mean crimes against public morality. Freud himself triggered a discussion of sexual child abuse within the family in an early article, "The Aetiology of Hysteria" (1962), which argued its prevalence, but soon afterwards reversed himself, emphasizing instead "infantile sexuality" and the role of sexual fantasies. What he had believed to be the actual sexual experiences of children were relegated to the world of childhood fantasies. Many psychoanalysts claim that this retraction, coupled with the discovery of the "Oedipus complex," was the actual beginning of psychoanalysis as a serious scientific enterprise. (See also Crews 1997 for the stormy debate surrounding the publication of Masson's book in 1984, which tries to document the historical events of this early episode in psychoanalysis.)

Whereas in France and Germany professionals studied the abuse of children in terms of a general moral decline related to modernity, sexual assaults against children in England and in the United States were discussed and fought against specifically in terms of the conditions of poverty, and especially of the housing conditions of the working class. The English debates prior to the Incest Act of 1908 demonstrate clearly that English public opinion and lawmakers viewed incest as a phenomenon manifesting itself only among the lower classes (Mearns 1883; Wohl 1978). In declaring that "incest is common" among the poor in London, Mearns shocked readers of his study of urban poverty, *The Bitter Cry of Outcast London,* published in 1883.

The sexual abuse of children was exposed and analyzed by feminist writers as part of their analysis of general patriarchal domination of women and children by men (Herman 1981; Rush 1980). Autobiographical accounts of sexual abuse and incest became more common (Armstrong 1978; Brady 1980; Hill 1985, among others). The feminist analysis did not emphasize class, but exchanged the class emphasis with an overall moral responsibility that saw all men as real or potential perpetrators of sexual abuse, another aspect of the process of universalization. Concepts like "incest" and "child molestation" were defined as "sexual abuse." The problem underlying all these was masculinity (see also MacLeod and Saraga 1988). The agenda of this conceptual shift has been to struggle against the formalization and universalization of child abuse.

The understanding of child abuse as sexual abuse has from the late 1970s taken center stage in the public perceptions of child abuse. The National Center on Child Abuse and Neglect introduced an official definition in 1981:

> Contact and interactions between a child and an adult when the child is being used for the sexual stimulation of the perpetrator or another person. Sexual abuse may also be committed by a person under the age of 18 when that person is either significantly older than the victim or when the perpetrator is in a position of power or control over another. (quoted in Hartman and Burgess 1989, 97)

Reported statistics on the prevalence of sexual abuse vary from 15 to 30 percent of all female children, and from 5 to 10 percent of all male children. All studies agree that sexual abuse is much more prevalent within the family than outside of it. However, much more difficult to substantiate than those of physical child abuse, the statistics regarding the prevalence of sexual abuse are highly controversial (Crewdson 1988; Hechler 1988). A pamphlet of the Parents League of the U.S. in 1986 exemplifies the point that sexual abuse has absorbed all definitions: "Think of five children you know. One will become the victim of child abuse. That's a fact we are trying to change. About one in five children are sexually abused . . . typically not once but repeatedly over a period of months or years" (quoted in Best 1990, 72).

Fears about sexual child abuse were also reinforced through television programs, fictional and nonfictional. For instance, in 1984 ABC broadcast the made-for-TV movie *Something about Amelia,* which is often rebroadcast on cable TV around the country. The movie depicted a white middle-class suburban family, wherein the father was engaged in an incestuous relationship with his little daughter. The movie received enormously high ratings, and after the broadcast child-abuse hotlines were flooded with calls about sexual abuse. Afternoon television shows frequently deal with the horrors of sexual child abuse. (From the late 1970s on, popular detective novels also started to take up the issue of child abuse, very often sexual in nature. On detective novels and child abuse, see Best 1990, 118–24.)

Public concern with child abuse in the last thirty years has been driven from one issue to another: the battering of children, sexual abuse, and ritual abuse. Sibling abuse and elderly abuse are being increasingly incorporated into the studies of family violence (Gelles 1990, 84ff).

SENTIMENTALIZATION AND COMPASSION

The modern liberal project attempted to emancipate citizens from traditional hierarchical forms of authority to implement a new sphere of individual freedom. This was partly accomplished by constituting the private sphere as a sphere of freedom, a place for intimate relationships. This private sphere was supposed to be independent of the political realm. Policies based on compassion, coupled with responsibility for the lives of those in the private sphere, must constantly cross the boundaries between these two spheres, because child abuse and neglect points to a breakdown of the possibilities of autonomy in this sphere. Hence, every public interference in this sphere is perceived as problematic in the sense that it destroys the autonomy of the family. As much as private love and compassion for children is taken for granted, public love and compassion in terms of national programs to aid children in distress are lagging far behind (Grubb and Lazerson 1982). Children through their increased sentimentalization are seen as emotional assets through which parents can realize themselves as private citizens. The emotional gratification that children provide as a means for parental fulfillment is reinforced by the child-abuse campaigns filtered through the public by the media. This campaign strengthens the emotional commitment of "normal" parents to their children as private assets. Public compassion in this case is redirected to strengthen private commitment. Note for instance the enormous popularity of the television series *Bradshaw on the Family*. Bradshaw has stretched the concept of child abuse to its outer limits in claiming that almost every form of child rearing, as the imposition of parental will over children, is emotionally damaging for the child (Bradshaw 1988). His ideas are based on the work of the Swiss psychoanalyst Alice Miller (1981, 1984, 1986), who also claims that education and child rearing in themselves are damaging to children's healthy emotional development and blames everything from fascism to other forms of authoritarian structures on bad parenting. Her and Bradshaw's central thesis can be summarized simply with the statement that child rearing is mental cruelty disguised in the form of love (see also Schatzman 1973; the German equivalent is Braunmühl 1975, 1978). This development can be understood partly as a result of the transition of democratic rhetoric into "democratic consumerism" (Hanson 1985, chapter 8). This means that the meaning and legitimacy of democracy in America is increasingly being linked to economic performance alone and the availability of consumer goods (Wolin 1981). Democratic rhetoric lost its ethical concern in defining what the good society is and concerned itself with the desire to do good without imposing any clear notion of what that good actually means. Compassion turned inward allows for indignation toward those who cause suffering and at the same time identification at low cost with sufferers. But it does not necessarily lead to public action. As a consequence, there is discontinuity in the moral language of liberalism, defining citizens' public responsibility for each other (Holmes 1988). Hanson sees the policies of the New Deal and its consequent emphasis on instrumentalism and "consumer democracy" as being the origin of the loss that left a moral vacuum:

> For it then becomes apparent that this rise of a conception of democracy that looks neither to the past nor to the future signified the relative decline of all ethical conceptions of democracy, regardless of their specific moral content. Henceforth, the meaning and legitimacy of democracy in America was linked to economic performance and the abundance of consumer goods, rather than moral achievement. (Hanson 1985, 258)

It seems that specialists in compassion have become highly selective in their choice of concern, especially in the face of the high rate of poor children in the United States and overwhelming evidence of the connection of poverty with child abuse and neglect. Studies point to the persistent poverty among children in the United States (Duncan 1991; Pelton 1989; Segal 1991; Wolock 1984). These studies are minute in comparison with the hundreds of studies published annually in the social-service journals on different kinds of child abuse and its treatment. Child neglect as the failure of caretakers to provide minimal adequate care, the predominant category of child maltreatment in the 1950s, is now completely dominated by the category of abuse, sexual or physical. Very few scholars assert that child mistreatment occurs to a greater degree among the poor. Most researchers working with a "disease" model assume that if the middle and upper classes were under more public scrutiny, the researchers would discover the real proportions of the "epidemic."

Compassion without an underlying moral language of solidarity is sentimentality and offers weak motivations for public action. The distinction between one's own and other people's children cannot be bridged by sentimentality alone. Especially from the 1970s on, negative attitudes toward other people's children have reinforced resistance to public programs supporting children (Grubb and Lazerson 1982; Keniston 1977; Kimmich 1985; Macchiarola and Gartner 1989). Fueled by racial biases, public compassion toward especially the children of the poor is embedded in a language that segregates parts of the American population increasingly from the pool of public sympathy. Federal aid in the form of Aid to Families with Dependent Children especially has become one of the more controversial programs in recent years. Not only are issues of child maltreatment ignored in this context, but as Thomas and Mary Edsall (1990) have recently argued, it seems that many members of the liberal establishment in the Democratic party and elsewhere shy away from problems of crime, sexual responsibility, welfare dependency, drug abuse, etc., for fear of being identified as racists or as "blaming the victim," leaving the ground for moral debate to conservatives. However, these are issues of legitimate political and moral debate. Without an open discussion of the social and racial components of child maltreatment, public compassion will indeed remain sentimental and private.

Conclusion

I have tried to show that compassion as moral sentiment and as humanitarian praxis exists. I used the example of children and the emergence of compassion toward them. But can we really claim that modern society is a compassionate society? Has our century not been the century of horror, mass extermination, genocide, the cruelest and most callous conduct mankind has ever seen? Do not the ovens of the extermination camps in the 1940s cry out that compassion is not a feature of modernity, especially argued by those who see the Holocaust even as the logical consequence of modernity? How can the attempt to curb violence against children compare to these horrors? Is it enough to just have a language that gives us the opportunity to recognize these horrors as such and cry out in lamentation about evil? Is that all that is left?

Clearly this has been the century of cruelty, and it also has been the century of compassion. If we understand the moral foundations of modern society as the interplay between compassion and barbarism that results from the world's moving between a communal morality and a universal one, then we will be able to see not only the breakdown of ethics but also its construction and the processes that accompany both of them. The French Revolution also played a key role in the history of compassion. It produced the Declaration of the Rights of Man, perhaps the founding document in the history of human rights, and in its armies the ideal of equality literally conquered Europe. But the French Revolution was also the site of horrific cruelty. How can these two things be reconciled? Hannah Arendt gives a direct answer: compassion has no place in politics, and when it enters, it leads to cruelty. She believes that modernity begins with the mobs of the French Revolution, and climaxes in the mobs of totalitarianism (Arendt 1963). For her, compassion is not politics. I have shown that it is. Compassion abolishes distance between people, so says Arendt (see also Canovan 1992 and Hansen 1993), but it is exactly distance that can create the kind of public compassion that Arendt would consider an oxymoron. Suffering people, children, animals do not have to be turned into abstract masses. The danger exists; sentimentality always lurks in the back of compassion, but it is not intrinsic to it. For Arendt, at the base of compassion is disdain for the real suffering of people. It is the cause that becomes important, the first step to totalitarianism. Compassion cannot make one free. Arendt might be right here. Compassion was not meant to make one free. But does it imprison us? Her theoretical influence empowered an entire tradition suspicious of modern forms of politics that do not share the high-mindedness of the Athenian polis. Arendt's line of thought comes to its consequence by trying to show not only how much totalitarianism is a sign of modernity, but even more: that the realm considered the evilest of all by most people, Nazi Germany and the concentration camps, the world where compassion ended, is a consequence of modernity. The entering of compassion into politics begot the most cruelty of all, the world of the concentration camp. Does that mean that the modern temperament is rather barbarian, as Mestrovic (1993) argues? Can the Holocaust be considered the breakdown of compassion? Is barbarism the true face of modernity? Thus, the critics of modernity argue, the breakdown of civilization is part and parcel of the processes of rationalization and bureaucratization. Arendt hinted to this view; Horkheimer and Adorno radicalized it in their *Dialectics of the Enlightenment* (1971). Foucault and Bauman continued this view of modernity. For Foucault (1965, 1977), humanitarian actions, which I analyzed above, are expressions of discipline and violence. For Bauman (1989), the attempt in modernity to create order—and public compassion does, of course, exactly that—is a form of violence with the worst consequences. But is this true? Can it not be argued that modernity is a form of consciousness and being that is aware of its potential for cruelty and that tries to overcome it in a process of civilization? But in order to do this, it needs concepts of civility, which in turn ask for the recognition of other people's suffering (i.e., compassion). Incomplete as it might be when faced with the cruelties of this world, this state of mind and action is only possible in a modernity of a special kind, namely in a democratic market society.

The question remains whether we talk about "modernity in general" or whether we talk about "peculiar German history" when talking about the Holocaust. I would like to suggest that "modernity" the way Bauman understands it is too weak a concept to try to encompass such an event as the Holocaust. This complete breakdown of civilization, and with it the breakdown of compassion, was first of all an event that involved Germans and Jews. The German Nazis identified themselves with the heroic life, which they contrasted with "Jewish parasites" and mundane everyday life. Nothing scared them more than the perceived decline of heroic ethics, which they identified—and rightly so—with the rise of commercial capitalism. But for them, commercial capitalism was embodied in the Jew. The decline of heroic ethics implied at the same time a "feminization" of culture. But the "feminization" of culture very often meant to the Nazis the Judaization of culture as well. Anti-Semitic imagery not only identified the Jew with the soulless spirit of capitalism, but also as an incomplete man, a woman actually. Hence, for many who identified the commercial spirit with a decline of manly heroism, the identification of Jews and women was almost complete. In more sophisticated forms, one can observe these tendencies in German sociology as well. The hatred of the bourgeois and his spirit was clear in the works of German social thinkers like Tönnies, Sombart, and Scheler, often mixed with anti-Semitism as well.

Elias, in his study titled *The Germans* (1996), points out that even during the end of the nineteenth and beginning of the twentieth century, the social status of rich bankers and merchants was significantly lower than that of high civil servants and military men. The predominance of the duel in German society is a case in point. Elias talks about the bourgeoisified warrior ethos of Wilhelmine German society. This military ethos was also dominant in the industrial spheres of lives. Many written testimonies speak about the parallels of running a factory with the same military discipline as running an army camp. This may not have been typical only for Germany, but there it was hegemonic. Opposed to this notion of Germanness rooted in the soil, defended by warriors ever willing to die an honorable death and fight without mercy and compassion, was the "homeless," the global, the commercial, in short, the "feminine" Jew. Remaining in the framework of Elias and his distinction between *"Kultur"* and *"Zivilisation,"* the Jew was representative of civilization and the German of culture. The Jew represented money and abstraction; in short, in the anti-Semitic German mind, the Jew stood for rootless capitalism. I have shown that one can think of money and "alienated" relations also in terms of impersonal relations between people. Obligations are anonymous and are turned into services. Money therefore tends to extend a concept of equality, insofar as the perception of inequality becomes based upon differences in person. This means that the predominance of money relations can unintentionally also foster moral relations like compassion between strangers. The analysis of the metropolis is a case in point. While it was Simmel (1900) who analyzed the "metropolis" as the site of freedom fostered by commercialized and depersonalized relations between people, the very same "metropolis" was analyzed by German sociologists like Sombart (1911) and Tönnies (1965) as the site of alienated and cold relations, as the site where Jews rule. Thus Sombart, in his *Jews and Capitalism*, wrote, "Now the modern city is nothing else but a great desert, as far removed from the warm earth as the desert is, and like it forcing its inhabitants to become nomads" (1911, 423, translation mine). And, of course, Sombart believed the Jews to be natural inhabitants of the desert, and by extension of the city. During Word War I, Sombart, in his *Händler und Helden* (Merchants and Heroes; 1915), took England to be the merchant nation (i.e., civilization) par excellence, while the Germans represented concrete heroism (i.e., culture).

Indeed, something different was going on in Germany. In *The Germans* (1996), Elias speaks about functional democratization, the emergence not only of a middle class, but of middle-class values. In Germany, the aristocratic concept of honor and glory outweighed bourgeois concepts of self-interested economic behavior. What I tried to show above is that a modern notion of compassion arises out of these bourgeois, so-called self-interested actions. Can we, therefore, speak of a German "special path" to history, a notion that seems to be increasingly discredited among historians and social scientists? I believe we should not dismiss Germany's "special path" right away. Elias (1996) talked about "honor" in the context of the duel, a habit that increasingly became discredited in countries outside of Germany as an atavistic residue of aristocratic conduct, while in Germany itself (as shown by Frevert 1991 and McAleer 1994) dueling became part of the habitus of a feudalized bourgeoisie. Clearly, honor and death are very much connected in the notion of the "honorable death." Honor is a positional good (in the words of Charles Taylor 1992); my honor is another's disgrace. My honorable death is somebody else's disgraceful death. Cassirer (1946) has shown how this aristocratic thinking is the bridge to racism and anti-Semitism. As Elias pointed out often enough in *The Germans,* the way from aristocratic to National Socialist concepts was short enough. While middle classes in other countries, especially in the Anglo-Saxon contexts, developed notions of institutionalized compassion, counteracting in many ways the brutalities and excesses of modern life and colonialism, in Germany the brutalization of the middle classes prevented this notion of compassion from emerging as a cultural value.

The major challenge to this view has been launched by Zygmunt Bauman. For Levinas (1990), the social is an extension of the interpersonal. Bauman (1989) misreads Levinas as propagating a presocial morality, a morality that withstands socialization, that withstands society. Levinas's "being with others" is transformed in Bauman to a moral principle that opposes socialization. By that, Bauman looks at the individual as outside of society, even as opposed to society. This view is ahistorical. It overlooks the historical and structural preconditions for the emergence of individualism (as was done by Elias 1978). Levinas (1990) speaks about the existential modality of interaction between people, a view that has been treated sociologically by Mead (1962), Elias (1978), and Habermas (1962). Bauman also "de-Judaizes" Levinas, neglecting completely the point that for Levinas ethics is Jewish ethics. Jewishness is the particularistic identity that is by nature universalistic. It is about religious identity. It is about identifying the deepest roots of Jewishness with modernity, not as something foreign, but as something the Jews invented. It is the antithesis to the above mentioned German habitus. Recall how Sombart compared the city to the desert and located the Jew in both those sites. As opposed to this, the German lives in the concrete forest. Forest and desert have been the archetypal opposites of Germans and Jews. This is true not only in the anti-Semitic mind. Levinas in *Difficult Freedom* (1990) tells us that the Jewish person discovers other people before he discovers landscapes. He is at home in a society before he is at home in a house. To be a Jew means to be free, to be disconnected, to be without roots. In the words of Levinas: "Man is no tree and mankind no forest" (36). This abstract relation to the other is confused by Bauman with an asociological point of view. Simmel, Mead, and Elias knew otherwise. And so did the Nazis.

What I want to say with all this is that it was not modernity that killed the Jews during the Holocaust in the most brutal manner. What killed the Jews was the direct opposite to their being, namely the Germans. To be a German meant first of all to be not a Jew. For Germans to be Germans, the Jew had to die, and not only die the normal death of an enemy, but a death without honor. A death without compassion. Think about how Jews were carried in wagons all over Europe for weeks just for the sole purpose of being killed. They were denied an "honorable death." I think Goldhagen (1996) in his very controversial study has put his finger on that. It was not "indifference" that killed the Jews, but an active, voluntaristic demand to torture and to annihilate them. Think of Auschwitz as a cosmopolitan society of uprooted Jews, speaking dozens of languages, having not much in common besides being Jews. This was the nightmarish civilization that German culture created. A world without compassion and without ethics. The very antithesis of modernity. To be modern means not to be barbaric. To be modern means to be able to recognize barbarism as such, to have a concept of it, to be able to name it. Compassion is key to this.

Bibliography

Abbott, Lyman. 1896. *Christianity and Social Problems*. Boston: Houghton.

Agnew, Jean-Christophe. 1986. *Worlds Apart: The Market and the Theater in Anglo-American Thought, 1550–1750*. Cambridge: Cambridge University Press.

American Humane Association. 1910. Thirty-Fourth Annual Report.

American Society for the Prevention of Cruelty to Animals. 1867. First Annual Report. New York.

Ames, James Barr. 1908. "Law and Morals." *Harvard Law Review* 22: 97–113.

Arendt, Hannah. 1958. *The Human Condition*. Chicago: University of Chicago Press.

———. 1963. *On Revolution*. New York: Viking.

Aries, Philippe. 1962. *Centuries of Childhood: A Social History of Family Life*. New York: Vintage.

Armstrong, Louise. 1978. *Kiss Daddy Goodnight*. New York: Hawthorne.

Bailey, Victor, and Sheila Blackburn. 1979. "The Punishment of Incest Act 1908: A Case Study of Law Creation." *Criminal Law Review*. 708–18.

Baker, Harvey. 1910. "Procedure of the Boston Juvenile Court." *The Survey* 23 (5 February): 643–50.

Baker, Paula. 1984. "The Domestication of Politics: Women and American Political Society, 1780–1920." *American Historical Review* 84:620–47.

Banerjee, Jacqueline. 1984. "Ambivalence and Contradictions: The Child in Victorian Fiction." *English Studies* 65:481–94.

Bauman, Zygmunt. 1989. *Modernity and the Holocaust*. Cambridge: Polity Press.

———. 1993. *Postmodern Ethics*. Oxford: Blackwell.

———. 1995. *Life in Fragments: Essays in Postmodern Moralities*. Oxford: Blackwell.

Beccaria, Cesare. 1986. *On Crimes and Punishments*. Reprint, Indianapolis: Hackett. Orig. pub. 1764.

Beck, Ulrich, ed. 1997a. *Kinder der Freiheit*. Frankfurt: Suhrkamp.

Beck, Ulrich. 1997b. "The Social Morality of an Individual Life." *Cultural Values* 1, no. 1:118–26.

Behlmer, George K. 1982. *Child Abuse and Moral Reform in England, 1870–1908*. Stanford: Stanford University Press.

Bellingham, Bruce. 1983. "The 'Unspeakable Blessing': Street Children, Reform Rhetoric, and Misery in Early Industrial Capitalism." *Politics and Society* 12:303–30.

Bender, Thomas. 1975. *Toward an Urban Vision.* Lexington: University Press of Kentucky.

Bentham, Jeremy. 1969. "An Introduction to the Principles of Morals and Legislation." In *British Moralists*, ed. D. D. Raphael. Reprint, Oxford: Oxford University Press. Orig. pub. 1789.

Berkenhoff, Hans Albert. 1937. *Tierstrafe, Tierbannung und Rechtsrituelle Tiertötung im Mittelalter.* Baden: Buhl.

Berlin, Isaiah. 1965. "Two Concepts of Liberty." In *Four Essays on Liberty.* New York: Oxford University Press.

Bernard, Paul. 1886. "Des Attentats a la pudeur et des violés sur les enfants. Legislation statistique." *Archives d'anthropologie criminelle et des sciences penales* 1:396–436.

Berry, Christopher. 1994. *The Idea of Luxury: A Conceptual and Historical Investigation.* Cambridge: Cambridge University Press.

Besharov, Douglas. 1990. *Recognizing Child Abuse: A Guide for the Concerned.* New York: Macmillan.

Best, Joel. 1990. *Threatened Children: Rhetoric and Concern about Child Victims.* Chicago: University of Chicago Press.

Bloch, Marc. 1961. *Feudal Society.* Reprint, Chicago: University of Chicago Press. Orig. pub. 1940.

Bloch, Ruth. 1978. "American Feminine Ideals in Transition: The Rise of the Moral Mother, 1785–1815." *Feminist Studies* 4:101–26.

Blumin, Stuart M. 1989. *The Emergence of the Middle Class: Social Experience in the American City, 1760–1900.* New York: Cambridge University Press.

Boli-Bennett, John, and John W. Meyer. 1978. "The Ideology of Childhood and the State: Rules Distinguishing Children in National Constitution, 1870–1970." *American Sociological Review* 43 (December):796–812.

Boltanski, Luc. 1993. *La Souffrance a Distance.* Paris: Metaille.

Boyer, Paul. 1978. *Urban Masses and Moral Order in America, 1820–1920.* Cambridge, Mass.: Harvard University Press.

Brace, Charles Loring. 1872. *The Dangerous Classes of New York.* New York: Wynkoop and Hallenbeck.

Bradshaw, John. 1988. *Bradshaw on: The Family.* Deerfield Beach, Fla.: Health Communications.

Brady, Catherine. 1980. *Father's Day.* New York: Seaview Books.

Braunmühl, Ekkehard von. 1975. *Antipädagogik.* Weinheim: Beltz.

———. 1978. *Zeit für Kinder.* Frankfurt: Fischer.

Breines, Wini, and Linda Gordon. 1983. "The New Scholarship on Family Violence." *Signs* 8, no. 3:490–531.

Bremner, Robert. 1964. *From the Depths: The Discovery of Poverty in the United States.* New York: New York University Press.

———, ed. 1970. *Children and Youth in America.* Vol. 1. Cambridge, Mass.: Harvard University Press.

———. 1971. *Children and Youth: A Documentary History.* Vol. 2, 1866–1932. Cambridge, Mass.: Harvard University Press.

Brinton, Crane. 1937. "Humanitarianism." In *The Encyclopedia of the Social Sciences.* Vol. 7. New York: Macmillan. 544–48.

————. 1959. *A History of Western Morals.* New York: Harcourt.

Brouardel, Paul. 1909. *Les Attentats aux Moeurs.* Paris: J. B. Bailliere.

Brunner, Otto. 1978. "Vom Ganzen Haus zur Familie." In *Seminar: Familie und Gesellschaftsstruktur,* ed. Heidi Rosenbaum. Frankfurt: Suhrkamp. 83–91.

Bushnell, Horace. 1967. *Christian Nurture.* Reprint, New Haven: Yale University Press. Orig. pub. 1847.

Caffey, John. 1946. "Multiple Fractures in the Long Bones of Infants Suffering from Subdural Hematoma." *American Journal of Roentgenology* 56:163–73.

Campbell, Colin. 1987. *The Romantic Ethic and the Sprit of Consumerism.* Oxford: Blackwell.

Canovan, Margaret. 1992. *Hannah Arendt: A Reinterpretation of Her Thought.* Cambridge: Cambridge University Press.

Carnes, Mark. 1990. "Middle-Class Men and the Solace of Fraternal Ritual." In *Meanings for Manhood: Constructions of Masculinity in Victorian America,* ed. Mark Carnes and Clyde Griffen. Chicago: University of Chicago Press. 37–52.

Carson, Gerald. 1972. *Men, Beasts, and Gods: A History of Cruelty and Kindness to Animals.* New York: Scribner.

Cartwright, David. 1984. "Kant, Schopenhauer, and Nietzsche on the Morality of Pity." *Journal of the History of Ideas* 45:83–98.

Casper, Johann Ludwig. 1863. *Klinische Novellen zur gerichtlichen Medizin.* Berlin: August Hirschwald.

Cassirer, Ernst. 1946. *The Myth of the State.* New Haven: Yale University Press.

Children's Aid Society. 1854–1860. Annual Reports (1–7). New York: Benedict.

Cladis, Mark. 1993. *A Communitarian Defense of Liberalism.* Stanford: Stanford University Press.

Clark, Clifford, Jr. 1976. "Domestic Architecture as an Index to Social History: The Romantic Revival and the Cult of Domesticity, 1840–1870." *Journal of Interdisciplinary History* 7:33–55.

Cobbe, Frances Power. 1878. "Wife-Torture in England." *The Contemporary Review* 32:55–87.

Cogan, Neil Howard. 1970. "Juvenile Law before and after the Entrance of 'Parens Patriae.'" *South Carolina Review* 22:147–81.

Coleman, Sydney. 1924. *Humane Society Leaders in America.* Albany: AHA.

Collini, Stefan. 1979. *Liberalism and Sociology: L. T. Hobhouse and Political Argument in England, 1880–1914.* Cambridge: Cambridge University Press.

Collins, Randall. 1974. "Three Faces of Cruelty: Toward a Comparative Sociology of Violence." *Theory and Society* 1:415–40.

Cooley, Charles Horton. 1962. *Social Organization.* Reprint, New York: Schocken. Orig. pub. 1909.

Costin, Lela. 1991. "Unravelling the Mary Ellen Legend: Origins of the 'Cruelty' Movement." *Social Service Review* 65:203–23.

Cott, Nancy. 1977. *The Bonds of Motherhood: Women's Sphere in New England, 1780–1835.* New Haven: Yale University Press.

————. 1978. "Divorce and the Changing Status of Women in Eighteenth-Century

Massachusetts." In *The American Family in Social-Historical Perspective*, ed. Michael Gordon. New York: St. Martin's Press. 115–39.

County Superintendents of the Poor of the State of New York. 1870–1895. Proceedings of Annual Conventions. Vols. 1–25.

Crane, S. R. 1934. "Suggestions toward a Genealogy of the 'Man of Feeling.'" *ELH: A Journal of English Literary History* 1:205–30.

Crewdson, John. 1988. *By Silence Betrayed: Sexual Abuse of Children in America*. Boston: Little Brown.

Crews, Frederic. 1997. *The Memory Wars*. London: Granta Books.

Danbom, David. 1987. *The World of Hope: Progressives and the Struggle for an Ethical Public Life*. Philadelphia: Temple University Press.

Daniel, Jessica. 1983. "Child Abuse and Accidents in Black Families: A Controlled Comparative Study." *American Journal of Orthopsychiatry* 53:645–53.

Davis, Samuel, and Mortimer Schwartz. 1987. *Children's Rights and the Law*. Lexington, Mass.: Lexington Books.

Degler, Carl. 1980. *At Odds: Women and the Family in America from the Revolution to the Present*. New York: Oxford University Press.

DeJong, Mary. 1986. "'I Want to Be Like Jesus': The Self-Defining of Evangelical Hymnology." *Journal of the American Academy of Religion* 54:461–93.

Delumeau, Jean. 1978. *La Peur en Occident*. Paris: Fayard.

Demos, John. 1970. *A Little Commonwealth: Family Life in Plymouth Colony*. New York: Oxford University Press.

Dewey, John. 1927. *The Public and Its Problems*. Chicago: Sage Books.

———. 1969. "The Ethics of Democracy." In *The Early Works, 1882–1898*. Reprint, Carbondale: Southern Illinois University Press, 227–49. Orig. pub. 1888.

Dickey, Lawrence. 1986. "Historicizing the 'Adam Smith Problem': Conceptual, Historiographical, and Textual Issues." *Journal of Modern History* 58:579–609.

Donzelot, Jacques. 1979. *The Policing of Families*. New York: Pantheon.

Douglas, Ann. 1977. *The Feminization of American Culture*. New York: Knopf.

Dudden, Faye. 1983. *Serving Women: Household Service in Nineteenth-Century America*. Middletown, Conn.: Wesleyan University Press.

Dülmen, Richard von. 1985. *Theater des Schreckens*. Munich: Beck.

Duncan, Greg. 1991. "Has Children's Poverty Become More Persistent?" *American Sociological Review* 56:538–50.

Durkheim, Émile. 1961. "The Use of Punishment in the School." In *Moral Education: A Study in the Theory and Application of the Sociology of Education*. Reprint, New York: Free Press, 182–83. Orig. pub. 1925.

———. 1964. *The Division of Labor in Society*. George Simpson, trans. Reprint, New York: Free Press. Orig. pub. 1893.

Eberle, Paul, and Shirley Eberle. 1986. *The Politics of Child Abuse*. Secaucus, N.J.: Lyle Stuart.

Edsall, Thomas, and Mary Edsall. 1990. *Chain Reaction: The Impact of Race, Rights, and Taxes on American Politics*. New York: Norton.

Elias, Norbert. 1978. *The Civilizing Process*. Edmund Jephcott, trans. Reprint, New York: Pantheon. Orig. pub. 1939.

———. 1996. *The Germans*. Cambridge: Polity Press.

Eliot, Thomas. 1914. *The Juvenile Court and the Community*. New York: Macmillan.

Encandela, John. 1993. "Social Science and the Study of Pain since Zbrowski: A Need for a New Agenda." *Social Science and Medicine* 36:783–91.

Epstein, Barbara Leslie. 1981. *The Politics of Domesticity: Women, Evangelism, and Temperance in Nineteenth-Century America.* Middletown, Conn.: Wesleyan University Press.

Etzioni, Amitai. 1994. *The Spirit of Community: The Reinvention of American Society.* New York: Simon and Schuster.

Evans, E. P. 1884. "Bugs and Beasts before the Law." *Atlantic Monthly* 55:235–46.

Farge, Arlette. 1986. *La Vie Fragile.* Paris: Hachette.

Farson, Richard. 1974. *Birthrights.* New York: Macmillan.

Feinberg, Joel. 1984. *Moral Limits of the Criminal Law.* Vol. 1, *Harm to Others.* New York: Oxford University Press.

Felt, Jeremy. 1965. *Hostages of Fortune: Child Labor Reform in New York State.* Syracuse, N.Y.: Syracuse University Press.

Fiering, Norbert. 1976. "Irresistible Compassion in the Eighteenth Century." *Journal of the History of Ideas* 27:195–218.

————. 1981. *Jonathan Edwards's Moral Thought and Its British Context.* Chapel Hill: University of North Carolina Press.

Fine, Sidney. 1956. *Laissez Faire and the General Welfare State: A Study of Conflict in American Thought, 1865–1901.* Ann Arbor: University of Michigan Press.

Fleming, Sanford. 1933. *Children and Puritanism: The Place of Children in the Life and Thought of New England Churches, 1620–1847.* New Haven: Yale University Press.

Fliegelman, Jay. 1982. *Prodigals and Pilgrims: The American Revolution against Patriarchal Authority, 1750–1800.* Cambridge: Cambridge University Press.

Folks, Homer. 1902. *The Care of Destitute, Neglected, and Delinquent Children.* New York: Macmillan.

Foucault, Michel. 1965. *Madness and Civilization.* New York: Random House.

————. 1977. *Discipline and Punish.* New York: Pantheon.

Franklin, Bob, ed. 1988. *The Rights of Children.* New York: Blackwell.

Freud, Sigmund. 1962. "The Aetiology of Hysteria." In *Complete Standard Edition.* Vol. 3. Reprint, London: Hogarth. Orig. pub. 1897. 189–221.

Frevert, Ute. 1991. "Bourgeois Honor: Middle Class Duelists in Germany from the Late Eighteenth Century to the Early Twentieth Century." In *The German Bourgeoisie*, ed. David Blackbourn and Richard J. Evans. London.

Fuchs, Rachel. 1983. "Crimes against Children in Nineteenth-Century France: Child Abuse." In *Law and Human Behavior* 6:237–59.

————. 1984. *Abandoned Children: Foundlings and Child Welfare in Nineteenth-Century France.* Albany: State University of New York Press.

Fuerth, Maria. 1933. *Caritas und Humanitas.* Stuttgart: Frommans Verlag.

Gatrell, V. A. C. 1994. *The Hanging Tree: Execution and the English People 1770–1868.* Oxford: Oxford University Press.

Gelles, Richard J. 1973. "Child Abuse as Psychopathology: A Sociological Critique and Reformulation." *American Journal of Orthopsychiatry* 43:611–21.

————. 1975. "The Social Construction of Child Abuse." *American Journal of Orthopsychiatry* 45:363–71.

————. 1985. "Family Violence." *Annual Review of Sociology* 11:347–67.

———. 1989. "Child Abuse and Violence in Single-Parent Families: Parent Absence and Economic Deprivation." *American Journal of Orthopsychiatry* 59:492–501.

Gelles, Richard, and Claire Cornell. 1990. *Intimate Violence in Families.* Newbury Park, Calif.: Sage.

Gellner, Ernst. 1992. *Postmodernism, Reason and Religion.* London: Routledge.

———. 1994. *Conditions of Liberty: Civil Society and Its Rivals.* London: Hamilton.

Gerry, Elbridge. 1883. "Cruelty to Children." *North American Review* 137:68.

———. 1895. "Must We Have the Cat-O-Nine Tails." *North American Review* 160 (March):318–24.

Gharpure, Narhar. 1935. *Tierschutz, Vegetarismus und Konfession.* München: Hohenhaus.

Gilder, George. 1981. *Wealth and Power.* New York: Basic Books.

Gilligan, Carol. 1982. *In a Different Voice.* Cambridge, Mass.: Harvard University Press.

Ginzberg, Lori. 1990. *Women and the Work of Benevolence: Morality, Politics, and Class in the Nineteenth-Century United States.* New Haven: Yale University Press.

Giovannoni, Jean M., and Rosian M. Becarra. 1979. *Defining Child Abuse.* New York: Free Press.

Goldhagen, Daniel Jona. 1996. *Hitler's Willing Executioners.* New York: Random House.

Goldstein, Joseph, Anna Freud, Albert J. Solnit. 1979. *Before the Best Interests of the Child.* New York: Free Press.

Gordon, Linda. 1988. *Heroes of Their Own Lives.* New York: Viking.

Gorrell, Donald. 1988. *The Age of Social Responsibility: The Social Gospel in the Progressive Era, 1900–1920.* Macon, Ga.: Mercer University Press.

Grady, John. 1983. "The Manufacture and Consumption of Child Abuse as a Social Issue." *Telos* 56:111–18.

Green, Harvey. 1983. *The Light of the Home: An Intimate View of the Lives of Women in Victorian America.* New York: Pantheon.

Green, T. H. 1986. "Lecture on Liberal Legislation and Freedom of Contract." In *Lectures on the Principles of Political Obligations and Other Writings,* ed. Paul Harris and John Morrow. Reprint, Cambridge: Cambridge University Press. 194–212. Orig. pub. 1881.

Greven, Philip. 1977. *The Protestant Temperament: Patterns of Child-Rearing, Religious Experience, and the Self in Early America.* Chicago: University of Chicago Press.

Grinwold, Richard. 1986a. "The Evolution of the Doctrine of Mental Cruelty in Victorian American Divorce, 1790–1900." *Journal of Social History* 20:127–48.

———. 1986b. "Law, Sex, Cruelty, and Divorce in Victorian America, 1840–1900." *American Quarterly* 38, no. 5:721–45.

Griswold, Robert. 1986. "Sexual Cruelty and the Case for Divorce in Victorian America." *Signs* 11, no. 3:529–41.

Grossberg, Michael. 1985. *Governing the Hearth: Law and Family in Nineteenth-Century America.* Chapel Hill: University of North Carolina Press.

Grubb, Norton, and Marvin Lazerson. 1982. *Broken Promises: How Americans Fail Their Children.* New York: Basic Books.

Habermas, Jürgen. 1962. *Strukturwandel der Öffentlichkeit.* Darmstadt: Neuwied.

Hacking, Ian. 1991. "The Making and Molding of Child Abuse." *Critical Inquiry* 17.

Hall, Robert. 1987. *Émile Durkheim: Ethics and the Sociology of Morals.* New York: Greenwood Press.

Halttunen, Karen. 1982. *Confidence Men and Painted Women: A Study of Middle-Class Culture in America, 1830–1870.* New Haven: Yale University Press.

———. 1995. "Humanitarianism and the Pornography of Pain in Anglo-American Culture." *American Historical Review* 100, no. 2:303–34.

Hampton, Robert. 1987. "Race, Class and Child Maltreatment." *Journal of Comparative Family Studies* 18:113–26.

Hanawalt, Barbara. 1976. "Violent Death in Fourteenth- and Early-Fifteenth-Century England." *Comparative Studies in Society and History* 18:297–320.

Hansen, Phillip. 1993. *Hannah Arendt: Politics, History and Citizenship*. Stanford: Stanford University Press.

Hanson, Russel. 1985. *The Democratic Imagination of the Past: Conversations with Our Past*. Princeton: Princeton University Press.

Hartman, Carol, and Ann Burgess. "Sexual Abuse of Children: Causes and Consequences." In *Child Maltreatment: Theory and Research on the Causes and Consequences of Child Abuse and Neglect*, ed. Dante Cichetti and Vicki Carlson. Cambridge: Cambridge University Press.

Harvey, David. 1989. *The Condition of Postmodernity*. Oxford: Blackwell.

Harwood, Dix. 1928. *Love for Animals and How It Developed in Great Britain*. New York: Columbia University Press.

Haskell, Thomas. 1977. *The Emergence of Professional Social Science: The American Social Science Association and the Nineteenth-Century Crisis of Authority*. Urbana: University of Illinois Press.

———. 1985. "Capitalism and the Origins of the Humanitarian Sensibility." Parts 1 and 2. *American Historical Review* 90:339–61, 547–66.

———. 1987. "Convention and Hegemonic Interest in the Debate over Antislavery: A Reply to Davis and Ashworth." *American Historical Review* 92:829–78.

Hawes, Joseph. 1971. *Children in Urban Society: Juvenile Delinquency in the Nineteenth Century*. New York: Oxford University Press.

Hechler, David. 1988. *The Battle and the Backlash: The Child Sexual Abuse War*. Lexington, Mass.: Lexington Books.

Helfer, Ray. 1987. "The Litany of the Smoldering Neglect of Children." In *The Battered Child*, 4th ed. ed. Ray Helfer and Ruth Kempe. Chicago: University of Chicago Press.

Herman, Judith. 1981. *Father–Daughter Incest*. Cambridge: Cambridge University Press.

Heuisler, Charles. 1903. "Probation Work in Children's Court." *Charities* 11:301–401.

Hicks, Robert. 1991. *In Pursuit of Satan: The Police and the Occult*. Buffalo: Prometheus Books.

Hill, Eleanore. 1985. *The Family Secret*. Santa Barbara: Rhodora Books.

Himmelfarb, Gertrude. 1991. *Poverty and Compassion: The Moral Imagination of the Late Victorians*. New York: Knopf.

Hiner, N. Ray. 1979. "Children's Rights, Corporal Punishment, and Child Abuse." *Bulletin of the Menninger Clinic* 43:239–40.

Hirsch, Fred. 1976. *Social Limits to Growth*. Cambridge, Mass.: Harvard University Press.

Hirschman, Albert. 1982. "Rival Interpretations of Market Society." *Journal of Economic Literature* 20:1463–84.

Hobhouse, L. T. 1964. *Liberalism*. Reprint, New York: Oxford University Press. Orig. pub. 1911.

Hobsbawm, E. J. 1975. *The Age of Capital 1848–1875*. New York: Scribner.

Hofstaedter, Richard. 1945. *Social Darwinism in American Thought*. Philadelphia: University of Pennsylvania Press.

Holmes, Stephen. 1988. "Liberal Guilt: Some Theoretical Origins of the Welfare State." In *Responsibility, Rights, and Welfare*, ed. J. Donald Moon. London: Westview Press. 77–106.

———. 1990. "The Secret History of Self-Interest." In *Beyond Self-Interest*, ed. Jane Mansbridge. Chicago: University of Chicago Press. 267–86.

Hopkins, Charles Howard. 1940. *The Rise of the Social Gospel in American Protestantism, 1865–1915*. New Haven: Yale University Press.

Horkheimer, Max, and Theodor Adorno. 1971. "Juliette oder Aufklärung und Moral." In *Dialektik der Aufklärung*. Reprint, Frankfurt: Fischer. 93. Orig. pub. 1944.

Horn, Margo. 1984. "The Moral Message of Child-Guidance." *Journal of Social History* 18:25–36.

Howe, David Walker. 1983. "The Social Science of Horace Bushnell." *Journal of American History*. 70:305–22.

Hubbard, Morse. 1915. "Prevention of Cruelty to Animals in New York State." *Bulletin of Social Legislation* 3.

Huizinga, Johan. 1954. *The Waning of the Middle Ages*. Reprint, New York: Doubleday. Orig. pub. 1924.

Hume, David. 1988. *An Enquiry Concerning the Principles of Morals*. Reprint, Indianapolis: Hackett. Orig. pub. 1751.

Humphrey, Gurteen S. 1882. *A Handbook of Charity Organization*. Buffalo: Pub. by the author.

Hyman, Irwin. 1990. *Reading, Writing, and the Hickory Stick*. Lexington, Mass.: Lexington Books.

Ignatieff, Michael. 1978. *A Just Measure of Pain: The Penitentiary in Industrial Society, 1750–1850*. London: Macmillan.

———. 1986. *The Needs of Strangers*. New York: Viking.

———. 1997. *The Warrior's Honor: Ethnic War and the Modern Conscience*. New York: Metropolitan Books.

Jacob, Margaret. 1976. *The Newtonians and the English Revolution: 1689–1720*. Ithaca: Cornell University Press.

Janowitz, Morris. 1975. "Sociological Theory and Social Control." *American Journal of Sociology* 81, no. 1:82–108.

Jasper, James, and Dorothy Nelkin. 1992. *The Animals Rights Crusade: The Growth of a Moral Crusade*. New York: Free Press.

Kant, Immanuel. 1991. *The Metaphysics of Morals*. Mary Gregor, intro., trans., and notes. Reprint, Cambridge: Cambridge University Press. Orig. pub. 1797.

Katz, Michael. 1983. *Poverty and Policy in American History*. New York: Academic Press.

———. 1986. *In the Shadow of the Poorhouse: A Social History of Welfare in America*. New York: Basic Books.

Kaus, Mickey. 1986. "Up from Altruism: The Case against Compassion." *New Republic*, 15 December: 17–18.

Kelley, Florence. 1905. *Some Ethical Gains through Legislation*. New York: Macmillan.

Kelly, Mary. 1979. "The Sentimentalists: Promise and Betrayal in the Home." *Signs* 4:434–46.

Kempe, Henry, Frederic Silverman, Brandt Steele, William Droegemueller, Henry Silver. 1962. "The Battered-Child Syndrome." *Journal of the American Medical Association* 181 (7 July):17–24.

Keniston, Kenneth. 1977. *All Our Children: The American Family under Pressure.* New York: Harvest.

Kimmich, Madeleine. 1985. *American Children: Who Cares?* Washington, D.C.: Urban Institute Press.

Kirchheimer, Otto. 1942. "Criminal Omissions." *Harvard Law Review* 55:615–42.

Kleinig, John. 1976. "Good Samaritanism." *Philosophy and Public Affairs* 5:382–407.

Kleinman, Arthur. 1992. "Pain as Human Experience: An Introduction." In *Pain as Human Experience: An Anthropological Perspective*, ed. Mary-Jo Delvecchio Good. Berkeley: University of California Press. 1–28.

Kloppenberg, James. 1986. *Uncertain Victory: Social Democracy and Progressivism in European and American Thought, 1870–1920.* New York: Oxford University Press.

Krafft-Ebing, Richard von. 1895. "Ueber Unzucht mit Kindern und Paedophilia erotica." In *Friedreichs Blaetter fuer gerichtliche Medizin.*

Krieken, Robert van. 1986. "Social Theory and Child Welfare." *Theory and Society* 15:401–29.

———. 1990. "The Organization of the Soul: Elias and Foucault on Discipline and the Self." *European Journal of Sociology* 31:353–71.

Kuczynski, Juergen. 1968. "Studien zur Geschichte der Lage des arbeitenden Kindes in Deutschland von 1700 bis zur Gegenwart." In *Geschichte der Lage der Arbeiter unter dem Kapitalismus.* Bd. 19. Berlin.

Kuhn, Anne L. 1947. *The Mother's Role in Childhood Education: New England Concepts 1830–1860.* New Haven: Yale University Press.

Lacassagne, Alexandre. 1886. "Attentats a la pudeur sur les petites filles." *Archives d'anthropologie criminelle et des sciences penales* 1:59–68.

Langbein, John. 1977. *Torture and the Law of Proof.* Chicago: University of Chicago Press.

Lasch, Christopher. 1977. *Haven in a Heartless World.* New York: Basic Books.

Lash, Scott. 1996. "Postmodern Ethics: The Missing Ground." *Theory, Culture and Society* 13, no. 2:91–104.

Lauritzen, Paul. 1989. "A Feminist Ethic and the New Romanticism: Mothering as a Model of Moral Relations." *Hypatia* 4:29–44.

Laws of New York State. 1881. Ch. 676. Abandonment and Other Acts of Cruelty to Children.

Leff, Mark. 1973. "Consensus for Reform: The Mothers'-Pension Movement in the Progressive Era." *Social Service Review* 47:397–417.

Leiby, James. 1978. *A History of Social Welfare and Social Work in the United States.* New York: Columbia University Press.

Levie, Dagobert. 1947. *The Modern Idea of the Prevention of Cruelty to Animals and Its Reflection in English Poetry.* New York: Vanni.

———. 1975. *Die Menschenliebe im Zeitalter der Aufklärung.* Bern: Lang Verlag.

Levinas, Emmanuel. 1990. *Difficult Freedom.* Baltimore: Johns Hopkins University Press.

Lipkin, Robert Justin. 1983. "Beyond Good Samaritan and Moral Monsters: An Individualistic Justification of the General Legal Duty to Rescue." *UCLA Law Review* 31:252–93.

Lowell, Josephine Shaw. 1884. *Public Relief and Public Charity.* New York: Putnam.

Lubove, Roy. 1969. *The Professional Altruist: The Emergence of Social Work as a Career, 1880–1930.* New York: Athenaeum.

————. 1986. *The Struggle for Social Security, 1900–1935.* Reprint, Pittsburgh: University of Pittsburgh Press. Orig. pub. 1968.

Lukacs, John. 1970. "The Bourgeois Interior." *American Scholar* 39:616–30.

Lyons, Arthur. 1988. *Satan Wants You: The Cult of Devil Worship in America.* New York: The Mysterious Press.

Macchiarola, Frank, and Alan Gartner, eds. 1989. *Caring for America's Children.* Proceedings of the Academy of Political Science. Vol. 37.

Macfarlane, Alan. 1978. *The Origins of English Individualism.* Oxford: Basil Blackwell.

MacIntyre, Alasdair. 1984. *After Virtue: A Study in Moral Theory.* Notre Dame: University of Notre Dame Press.

MacLeod, Mary, and Esther Saraga. 1988. "Challenging the Orthodoxy: Toward a Feminist Theory and Practice." *Feminist Review* 28:16–55.

MacPherson, C. B. 1973. *Democratic Theory: Essays in Retrieval.* Oxford: Clarendon Press.

Maffesoli, Michel. 1995. *The Time of the Tribes: The Decline in Individualism in Mass Society.* London: Sage.

Manufacturers' Record. 1924. "What the Child Labor Amendment Means." September 4.

Margolin, C. R. 1978. "Salvation versus Liberation: The Movement for Children's Rights in Historical Context." *Social Problems* 25, no. 4 (April):441–52.

Marx, Karl. 1972. "Manifesto of the Communist Party." In *The Marx-Engels Reader*, ed. Robert Tucker. New York: Norton. 475.

Masson, Jeffrey M. 1984. *The Assault on Truth.* New York: Penguin.

Matthews, Fred. 1988. "The Utopia of Human Relations: The Conflict-Free Family in American Social Thought, 1930–1960." *Journal of the History of Behavioral Sciences* 24:343–62.

McAleer, Kevin. 1994. *Duelling: The Cult of Honor in Fin-de-Siecle Germany.* Princeton: Princeton University Press.

McCrea, Roswell. 1910. *The Humane Movement.* New York: Columbia University Press.

McElvaine, Robert. 1981. *The Great Depression.* New York: Random House.

Mead, George Herbert. 1962. *Mind, Self and Society.* Chicago: University of Chicago Press.

Mead, Lawrence. 1986. *Beyond Entitlement: The Social Obligations of Citizenship.* New York: Macmillan.

Mearns, Andrew. 1970. *The Bitter Cry of Outcast London.* Reprint, Leicester: Leicester University Press. Orig. pub. 1883.

Mennel, Robert. 1973. *Thorns and Thistles: Juvenile Delinquents in the United States.* Hanover: University of New Hampshire Press.

Mestrovic, Stjepan. 1988. *Émile Durkheim and the Reformation of Sociology.* Totowa, N.J.: Rowman and Littlefield.

————. 1993. *The Barbarian Temperament.* London: Routledge.

————. 1997. *Postemotional Society.* London: Sage.

Meyer, Philippe. 1983. *The Child and the State: The Intervention of the State in Family Life.* Cambridge: Cambridge University Press.

Mill, John Stuart. 1976. *On Liberty.* Reprint, Oxford: Oxford University Press. Orig. pub. 1859.

————. 1975. "The Subjection of Women." In *Three Essays.* Reprint, Oxford: Oxford University Press. Orig. pub. 1869

Miller, Alice. 1981. *The Drama of the Gifted Child.* Reprint, New York: Basic Books. Orig. pub. 1979.

———. 1984. *For Your Own Good: Hidden Cruelty in Child Rearing and the Roots of Violence.* Reprint, New York: Farrar, Straus and Giroux. Orig. pub. 1980.

———. 1986. *Thou Shalt Not Be Aware.* Reprint, New York: Meridan. Orig. pub. 1981.

Miller, James. 1990. "Carnivals of Atrocity: Foucault, Nietzsche, Cruelty." *Political Theory.* 18:470–91.

Mizuta, Hiroshi. 1975. "Moral Philosophy and Civil Society." In *Essays on Adam Smith,* ed. Andrew Skinner and Thomas Wilson, eds. Oxford: Clarendon Press. 114—31.

Mnookin, H. R. 1973. "Foster Care: In Whose Best Interest?" *Harvard Educational Review* 43:599–638.

Morgan, Edmund. 1966. *The Puritan Family: Religion and Domestic Relations in Seventeenth-Century New England.* Reprint, Westport, Conn.: Greenwood Press. Orig. pub. 1944.

Morris, David. 1991. *The Culture of Pain.* Berkeley: University of California Press.

Muchembled, Robert. 1989. *La Violence en Occident.* Turnhout, Belgium: Editions Brepols.

Murray, Charles. 1984. *Losing Ground: American Social Policy, 1950–1980.* New York: Basic Books.

Musewicz, J. J. 1981. "The Failure of Foster Care: Federal Statutory Reform and the Child's Right to Permanence." *Southern California Law Review* 54:633–65.

Myers, John. 1985. "The Legal Response to Child Abuse: In the Best Interest of Children?" *Journal of Family Law* 242:149–269.

Nadelhaft, Jerome. 1987. "Wife Torture: A Known Phenomenon in Nineteenth-Century America." *Journal of American Culture* 10:39–59.

Nelson, Barbara. 1984. *Making an Issue of Child Abuse: Political Agenda Setting for Social Problems.* Chicago: University of Chicago Press.

Nelson, Benjamin. 1949. *The Ideal of Usury: From Tribal Brotherhood to Universal Otherhood.* Princeton: Princeton University Press.

Neuman, R. O. 1975. "Masturbation, Madness, and the Modern Concepts of Childhood and Adolescence." *Journal of Social History* 8 (Spring):127.

New York Society for the Prevention of Cruelty to Children. 1875–1934. Annual Reports 1–60.

New York Times. 1896. January 12.

Niebuhr, Reinhold. 1956. *An Interpretation of Christian Ethics.* New York: Meridan.

Nietzsche, Friedrich. 1968. *On the Genealogy of Morals.* Reprint, New York: Vintage. Orig. pub. 1887.

Nisbet, Robert. 1961. "The Study of Social Problems." In *Contemporary Social Problems,* ed. Robert Merton and Robert Nisbet. New York: Harcourt Brace. 1–25.

———. 1966. *The Sociological Tradition.* New York: Basic Books.

Noddings, Nel. 1984. *Caring: A Feminine Approach to Ethics and Moral Education.* Berkeley: University of California Press.

Norton, Mary Beth. 1984. "The Evolution of White Women's Experience in Early America." *American Historical Review* 89:593–619.

Nuechterlein, James. 1987. "The Feminization of the American Left." *Commentary* 84, no. 5 (November):43–48.

Nygren, Anders. 1953. *Agape and Eros.* Reprint, Philadelphia: Westminster Press. Orig. pub. 1938.

Oestreich, Gerhard. 1969. *Geist und Gestalt des Frühmodernen Staates*. Berlin: Duncker und Humbolt.

Offe, Claus. "Democracy against the Welfare State? Structural Foundations of Neoconservative Political Opportunities." In *Responsibility, Rights, and Welfare: The Theory of the Welfare State*, ed. J. Donald Moon. London: Westview Press. 189–228.

Olk, Thomas and Rolf Heinze. 1981. "Die Buerokratisierung der Naechstenliebe." In *Jahrbuch der Sozialarbeit*, ed. Christoph Sachsse and Florian Tennstedt. Hamburg: Rowohlt. 233–271.

Oncken, August. 1897. "The Consistency of Adam Smith." *Economic Journal* 7:443–50.

Orwin, Clifford. 1980. "Compassion." *American Scholar* (Summer): 309–33.

———. 1996. "Distant Compassion: CNN and Borrioboola-Gha." *The National Interest* (Spring):42–49.

Ossowska, Maria. 1986. *Bourgeois Morality*. London: RKP.

Parton, Nigel. 1985. The *Politics of Child Abuse*. London: Macmillan.

Passmore, John. 1975. "The Treatment of Animals." *Journal of the History of Ideas* 36:195–218.

Pelton, Leroy. 1978. "Child Abuse and Neglect: The Myth of Classlessness." *American Journal of Orthopsychiatry* 48:608–17.

———. 1989. *For Reasons of Poverty: A Critical Analysis of the Public Child Welfare System in the United States*. New York: Praeger.

Pernick, Martin. 1985. *A Calculus of Suffering: Pain, Professionalism, and Anesthesia in Nineteenth-Century America*. New York: Columbia University Press.

Peters, Edward. 1985. *Torture*. New York: Blackwell.

Peters, Richard. 1973. *Reason and Compassion*. London: RKP.

Peukert, Detlev. 1986. *Grenzen der Sozialdisziplinierung: Aufstieg und Krise der deutschen Jugendfuersorge*. Koeln: Bund Verlag.

Phillips, Derk. 1986. *Toward a Just Social Order*. Princeton: Princeton University Press.

Piven, Frances, and Richard Cloward. 1972. *Regulating the Poor*. London: Tavistock.

Platt, Anthony. 1977. *The Child Savers*. Chicago: University of Chicago Press.

Pleck, Elizabeth H. 1983. "Feminist Responses to 'Crimes against Women,' 1868–1896." *Signs* 8, no. 3:451–70.

———. 1987. *Domestic Tyranny: The Making of Social Policy against Family Violence from Colonial Times to the Present*. New York: Oxford University Press.

Poggi, Gianfranco. 1978. *The Development of the Modern State*. Stanford: Stanford University Press.

Price, David. 1974. "Community and Control: Critical Democratic Theory in the Progressive Period." *American Political Science Review* 68:1663–78.

Radner, John. 1979. "The Art of Sympathy in Eighteenth-Century British Moral Thought." *Studies in Eighteenth-Century Culture* 9:189–210.

Raschke, Carl. 1990. *Painted Black: From Drug Killings to Heavy Metal*. New York: Harper and Row.

Rauschenbusch, Walter. 1907. *Christianity and the Social Crisis*. New York: Macmillan.

———. 1912. *Christianizing the Social Order*. New York: Macmillan.

Reynolds, David. 1980. "The Feminization Controversy: Sexual Stereotypes and the Paradoxes of Piety in Nineteenth-Century America." *New England Quarterly* 53:96–106.

Richardson, James, Joel Best, David Bromley, eds. 1991. *The Satanism Scare*. New York: Gruyter.

Richmond, Mary. 1907. *Friendly Visiting among the Poor: A Handbook for Charity Workers.* New York: Macmillan.

Riis, Jacob. 1892. *The Children of the Poor.* New York: Scribner.

Ritvo, Harriet. 1987. *The Animal Estate: The English and Other Creatures in the Victorian Age.* Cambridge, Mass.: Harvard University Press.

Rodham, Hillary. 1973. "Children under the Law." *Harvard Educational Review* 43:487–515.

Rorty, Amélie Oksenberg. 1982. "From Passion to Emotions and Sentiments." *Philosophy* 57:159–172.

Rorty, Richard. 1989. *Contingency, Irony, and Solidarity.* New York: Cambridge University Press.

Rosenbaum, Heidi. 1982. *Formen der Familie.* Frankfurt: Suhrkamp.

Rosenberg, Charles. 1980. "Sexuality, Class and Role in Nineteenth-Century America." In *The American Man,* ed. Elizabeth Pleck and Joseph Pleck. Englewood Cliffs, N.J.: Prentice-Hall. 219–54.

Rosenberg, Martin. 1985. "The Alternative of Reward and Praise: The Case against a Duty to Rescue." *Columbia Journal of Law and Social Problems* 19:1–17.

Rosenberger, Alvin, and Eli Newberger. 1979. "Compassion vs. Control: Conceptual and Practical Pitfalls in the Broadened Definition of Child Abuse." In *Critical Perspectives on Child Abuse,* ed. Richard Bourne and Eli Newberger. Lexington, Mass.: Lexington Books. 81–87.

Rosenthal, A. M. 1964. *Thirty-Eight Witnesses.* New York: McGraw-Hill.

Ross, Edward Allsworth. 1910. *Social Control.* New York: Macmillan.

Rothman, David. 1971. *The Discovery of the Asylum.* Boston: Little Brown.

———. 1980. *Conscience and Convenience: The Asylum and Its Alternative in Progressive America.* Boston: Little Brown.

Rothman, Sheila. 1978. *Woman's Proper Place: A History of Changing Ideals and Practices, 1870 to the Present.* New York: Basic Books.

Rotundo, Anthony. 1987. "Learning about Manhood: Gender Ideals and the Middle-Class Family in Nineteenth-Century America." In *Manliness and Morality: Middle-Class Masculinity in Britain and America 1800–1940,* ed. J. A. Mangan and James Walvin. New York: St. Martin's Press. 35–51.

Rouche, Michel. 1987. "The Early Middle Ages in the West." In *A History of Private Life.* Vol. 1. Cambridge, Mass.: Harvard University Press. 411–549.

Rousseau, Jean-Jacques. 1979. *Émile, or On Education.* Reprint, New York: Basic Books. 221. Orig. pub. 1762.

Rush, Florence. 1980. *The Best-Kept Secret: The Sexual Abuse of Children.* New York: McGraw-Hill.

Ruthven, Malise. 1978. *Torture: The Grand Conspiracy.* London: Weidenfeld and Nicolson.

Rybczynski, Witold. 1986. *Home: A Short History of an Idea.* Middlesex: Penguin.

Ryerson, Ellen. 1978. *The Best-Laid Plans: America's Juvenile Court Experiment.* New York: Hill and Wang.

Salt, Henry. 1891. "Humanitarianism: Its General Principle and Progress." In *Cruelties of Civilization.* London: Humanitarian League's Publication.

———. 1894. *Animals' Rights.* New York: Macmillan.

Schatzman, Morton. 1973. *Soul Murder: Persecution in the Family.* New York: Random House.

Scheler, Max. 1972. *Das Ressentiment im Aufbau der Moralen.* Reprint, Frankfurt: Klostermann. Orig. pub. 1924.

Scherpner, Hans. 1966. *Geschichte der Jugendfürsorge* Göttingen: Vandenhoeck and Ruprecht.

Schlatter, Richard. 1971. *The Social Ideas of Religious Leaders: 1660–1688.* Reprint, New York: Octagon Books. Orig. pub. 1940.

Schlossman, Steven. 1977. *Love and the American Delinquent: The Theory and Practice of "Progressive" Juvenile Justice, 1825–1920.* Chicago: University of Chicago Press.

Schneider, David and Albert Deutsch. 1941. *The History of Public Welfare in New York State, 1867–1940.* Chicago: University of Chicago Press.

Schöffler, Herbert. 1922. *Protestantismus und Literatur: Neue Wege zur Englischen Literatur des Achtzehnten Jahrhunderts.* Leipzig: Tauchnitz.

Schopenhauer, Arthur. 1977. "Über die Grundlage der Moral." In *Kleine Schriften II.* Reprint, Zurich: Diogenes Verlag. Orig. pub. 1840.

Schumpeter, Joseph. 1942. *Capitalism, Socialism and Democracy.* New York: Harper.

Schwab, Dieter. 1971. "Die Rechtliche Stellung des Kindes in Geschichte und Gegenwart." In *Das Kind: Eine Anthropologie des Kindes,* ed. Wolfgang Behler. Freiburg: Herder. 379–406.

Segal, Elizabeth. 1991. "The Juvenilization of Poverty in the 1980s." *Social Work* 36:454–57.

Seligman, Adam. 1992. *The Idea of Civil Society.* New York: Free Press.

Sennett, Richard. 1974. *The Fall of Public Man.* New York: Knopf.

Shanley, Mary Lyndon. 1981. "Marital Slavery and Friendship," *Political Theory* 9:229–247.

Sheleff, Leon. 1978. *The Bystander: Behavior, Law, Ethics.* Lexington, Mass.: Lexington Books.

Shultz, William. 1924. *The Humane Movement in the United States, 1910–1922.* New York: AMS Press.

Sigourney, Lydia. 1854. *The Western Home and Other Poems.* Philadelphia: Perry & MacMillan.

Silver, Allan. 1990a. "The Curious Importance of Small Groups in American Sociology." In *Sociology in America,* ed. Herbert Gans. Newbury Park, Calif.: Sage. 66–67.

———. 1990b. "Friendship in Commercial Society: Eighteenth-Century Social Theory and Modern Society." *American Journal of Sociology* 95, no. 6:1474–1504.

Simmel, Georg. 1900. *Philosphie des Geldes.* Berlin: Humbolt.

Sklar, Kathryn Kish. 1973. *Catherine Beecher: A Study in American Domesticity.* New Haven: Yale University Press.

Skocpol, Theda. 1992. *Protecting Soldiers and Mothers.* Cambridge, Mass.: Harvard University Press.

Slater, Peter. 1977. *Children in the New England Mind in Death and in Life.* New York: Archon Books.

Smith, Adam. 1759. *The Theory of Moral Sentiments.* London: Milar.

Smith, Eva. 1987. "The Failure of the Destitute Mothers' Bill: The Use of Political Power in Social Welfare." *Journal of Sociology and Social Welfare* 14, no. 2:63–87.

Smith, Shelton H. 1955. *Changing Conceptions of Original Sin.* New York: Scribner.

Smith Rosenberg, Caroll. 1971. *Religion and the Rise of the American City: The New York City Mission Movement, 1812–1870.* Ithaca: New York State University Press.

———. 1985. *Disorderly Conduct.* New York: Oxford University Press.

Snow, Nancy. 1991. "Compassion." *American Philosophical Quarterly* 28:195–205.

Sombart, Werner. 1911. *Die Juden und das Wirtschaftsleben.* Leipzig: Duncker.

———. 1915. *Händler und Helden.* München: Duncker.

Sommerville, C. John. 1982. *The Rise and Fall of Childhood.* New York: Vintage.

Spargo, John. 1906. *The Bitter Cry of the Children.* New York: Macmillan.

Spierenburg, Peter. 1984. *The Spectacle of Suffering: Executions and the Evolution of Repression: From a Pre-Industrial Metropolis to the European Experience.* Cambridge: Cambridge University Press.

Stansell, Christine. 1982. "Women, Children, and the Uses of the Street: Class and Gender Conflicts in New York City, 1850–1860." *Feminist Studies* 8:309–35.

State Aid Charities. 1896. Annual Report.

Stearns, Peter. 1979. "The Middle Class: Toward a Precise Definition." *Comparative Studies of Society and History* 21:377–96.

Steele, Brandt. 1987. "Psychodynamic Factors in Child Abuse." In *The Battered Child,* 4th ed., ed. Ray Helfer and Henry Kempe. Chicago: University of Chicago Press.

Steele, Zulma. 1942. *Angel in Top Hat.* New York: Harper.

Stone, Lawrence. 1979. *The Family, Sex and Marriage in England 1500–1800.* New York: Harper.

Strauss, Leo. 1950. *Natural Rights and History.* Chicago: University of Chicago Press.

Sullivan, William. 1982. *Reconstructing Public Philosophy.* Berkeley: University of California Press.

Swaan, Abram de. 1981. "The Politics of Agoraphobia: On Changes in Emotional and Relational Management." *Theory and Society* 10:359–85.

———. 1988. *In Care of the State.* Oxford: Polity Press.

———. 1990. "Intimate Relations and Domestic Arrangements: Notes on the Sociogenesis of Intimacy." In *The Management of Normality.* London: RKP. 182–94.

Tardieu, Ambroise A. 1878. *Étude Medicolegale sur les Attentats aux moeurs.* Paris: J. B. Balliere.

Taylor, Charles. 1992. *The Ethics of Authenticity.* Cambridge, Mass.: Harvard University Press.

Thigpen, Robert, and Lyle Downing. 1987. "Liberalism and the Communitarian Critique." *American Journal of Political Science* 31:637–55.

Thomas, Keith. 1983. *Man and the Natural World: A History of Modern Sensibility.* New York: Pantheon.

Thomas, Mason P. 1972. "Child Abuse and Neglect: Historical Overview, Legal Matrix, and Social Perspective." *North Carolina Law Review* 50:293–349.

Thompson, F. M. L. 1981. "Social Control in Victorian Britain." *Economic History Review* 12:189–208.

Tiffin, Susan. 1982. *In Whose Best Interest? Child Welfare Reform in the Progressive Era.* Westport, Conn.: Greenwood Press.

Tocqueville, Alexis de. 1969. *Democracy in America.* Reprint, New York: Anchor Books. Orig. pub. 1840.

Tönnies, Ferdinand, 1965. *Community and Society.* Reprint, New York: Harper. Orig. pub. 1887.

Trattner, Walter. 1968. *Homer Folks: Pioneer in Social Welfare.* New York: Columbia University Press.

———. 1970. *Crusade for the Children: A History of the National Child Labor Committee and Child Labor Reform in America.* Chicago: Quadrangle Books.

———. 1989. *From Poor Law to Welfare State: A History of Social Welfare in America.* New York: Macmillan.

Turner, Bryan, ed. 1990. *Theories of Modernity and Postmodernity.* London: Sage.

Turner, James. 1980. *Reckoning with the Beast: Animals, Pain, and Humanity in the Victorian Mind.* Baltimore: Johns Hopkins University Press.

United Nations. 1960. *Declarations of the Rights of the Child.* Official Records of the General Assembly, Fourteenth Session. Supplement No. 16.

U.S. Senate. 1909. Conference on Care of Dependent Children. Proceedings. 60th Cong., 2d Sess.

U.S. Senate. 1973. Hearings before the Subcommittee on Children and Youth of the Committee on Labor and Public Welfare. 93d Cong., 1st Sess.

Vidich, Arthur, and Stanford Lyman. 1985. *American Sociology: Worldly Rejections of Religion and Their Directions.* New Haven: Yale University Press.

Walker, Samuel. 1990. *In Defense of American Liberties: A History of the ACLU.* New York: Oxford University Press.

Walzer, Michael. 1988. *The Company of Critics: Social Criticism and Political Commitment in the Twentieth Century.* New York: Basic Books.

Warner, Sam Bass Jr. 1968. *The Private City: Philadelphia in Three Periods of Its Growth.* Philadelphia: University of Pennsylvania Press.

Weber, Max. 1968. *Economy and Society: An Outline of Interpretative Sociology.* New York: Bedminster Press.

Weiss, Nancy. 1977. "Mother, the Invention of Necessity: Dr. Benjamin Spock's Baby and Child Care." *American Quarterly* 29:519–46.

Weissbach, Lee Shai. 1989. *Child Labor Reform in Nineteenth-Century France.* Baton Rouge: Louisiana State University Press.

Welter, Barbara. 1966. "The Cult of True Womanhood: 1820–1860." *American Quarterly* (Summer): 151–74.

Wexler, Richard. 1991. *Wounded Innocents: The Real Victims of the War against Child Abuse.* Buffalo: Prometheus.

Wheeler, Angell. 1913. "The Beginning of Child Protection: The Case of Mary Ellen as Told by Her Rescuer, Mrs. Etta Angell Wheeler." *National Humane Review*, (August): 183.

Wiebe, Robert. 1967. *The Search for Order, 1877–1920.* New York: Hill and Wang.

Wishy, Bernard. 1968. *The Child and the Republic: The Dawn of Modern American Child Nurture.* Philadelphia: University of Pennsylvania Press.

Wohl, Anthony. 1978. "Sex and the Single Room: Incest among the Victorian Working Classes." In *The Victorian Family: Structure and Stresses,* ed. Anthony Wohl. London: Croom Helm, 197–216.

Wolfe, Alan. 1989. *Whose Keeper? Social Science and Moral Obligation.* Berkeley: University of California Press.

Wolfram, Sybil. 1983. "Eugenics and the Punishment of Incest Act 1908." *Criminal Law Review.* 308–16.

Wolin, Sheldon. 1960. *Politics and Vision.* New York: Little Brown.

————. 1981. "The New Public Philosophy." *Democracy* 1:23–36.

Wolock, Isabel. 1984. "Child Maltreatment as a Social Problem: The Neglect of Neglect." *American Journal of Orthopsychiatry* 34:530–43.

Wright, Gwendolyn. 1980. *Moralism and the Model Home.* Chicago: University of Chicago Press.

————. 1981. *Building the Dream: A Social History of Housing in America.* New York: Pantheon.

Wringe, C. A. 1981. *Children's Rights: A Philosophical Study.* London: RKP.

Wuthrow, Robert. 1991. *Acts of Compassion: Caring for Others and Helping Ourselves.* Princeton: Princeton University Press.

Zbrowski, Mark. 1969. *People in Pain.* San Francisco: Jossey-Bass.

Zelizer, Viviana. 1985. *Pricing the Priceless Child: The Changing Social Value of Children.* New York: Basic Books.

Zenz, Gisela. 1979. *Kindermisshandlungen und Kindesrechte.* Frankfurt: Suhrkamp.

Index

123

About the Author

Natan Sznaider is currently Senior Lecturer in Sociology at the Academic College of Tel Aviv–Yaffo in Israel. He received his Ph.D. in sociology from Columbia University in New York. His research interests are the sociology of moral sentiments and the sociology of culture, in which he has published various articles and studies in Israel, Germany, and the United States.